NO OUTSIDERS: EVERY(
EVERYONE WE

CW00566309

The No Outsiders programme promotes an ethos of inclusion and tolerance, and aims to prepare children for life in modern Britain. Expanding the scheme published in the 2015 book, *No Outsiders in Our Schools*, this book is designed to further support educators as they make the No Outsiders ethos part of their school culture at a time when messages of fear and division are rife. Written by a practising teacher whose work to promote equality has been globally celebrated, this book provides lesson plans for use in classes from EYFS to Year 6.

Key features of the resource include:

- plans for delivering the No Outsiders message through assemblies and classes, allowing for a flexible approach

- recommendations for picture books that can be used to support messages of diversity and inclusion

- a scheme of work designed to meet the requirements of the Equalities Act (2010) and support teachers as they prepare to implement the new Relationships Education curriculum (2020).

It is the responsibility of primary schools to promote equality and diversity. This is a vital resource for all teachers and trainee teachers as they prepare children for a life where diversity is embraced and there is no fear of difference.

Andrew Moffat qualified as a teacher in 1996, taking up a position as a Year 1 class teacher in Derby. Since then Andrew has worked in a behaviour unit, a Nurture group, as an AST in behaviour management and inclusion, as manager of a behaviour resource in a primary school and, since 2014, as Assistant Headteacher at Parkfield Community School in Birmingham. Andrew is a qualified SENCo and also has a MEd in emotional and behavioural difficulties.

In 2015 *No Outsiders in Our School: Teaching the Equality Act in Primary Schools* was published and Andrew began training schools in using the resource to teach community cohesion. In 2016 Ofsted rated Parkfield Community School as 'Outstanding' and recognised No Outsiders as a key strength. In 2017 Andrew was awarded an MBE for equality and diversity work in education and in 2019 he was listed as a top 10 finalist in the Varkey Foundation Global Teacher Prize.

Andrew's work made national headlines in 2019 as it became the focus of protests against the inclusion of LGBT equality in primary schools. As a result, No Outsiders gained a national reputation; Andrew was listed in the Attitude Pride Awards 2019 and named Role Model of the year 2019 by Pink News. He was awarded an honorary doctorate by the University of Worcester and was named Hero of the Year in the 2019 European Diversity Awards.

Andrew continues to work full time as Assistant Headteacher at Parkfield Community School. He is founder and CEO of the No Outsiders charity and is also studying part time for a PhD at the University of Birmingham.

NO OUTSIDERS: EVERYONE DIFFERENT, EVERYONE WELCOME

Preparing Children for Life in Modern Britain

ANDREW MOFFAT

Routledge
Taylor & Francis Group

LONDON AND NEW YORK

First published 2020
by Routledge
2 Park Square, Milton Park, Abingdon, Oxon OX14 4RN

and by Routledge
52 Vanderbilt Avenue, New York, NY 10017

Routledge is an imprint of the Taylor & Francis Group, an informa business

© 2020 Andrew Moffat

British Library Cataloguing-in-Publication Data
A catalogue record for this book is available from the British Library

Library of Congress Cataloging-in-Publication Data
Names: Moffat, Andrew (Teacher), author.
Title: No outsiders : everyone different, everyone welcome :
preparing children for life in modern Britain / Andrew Moffat.
Description: First Edition. | New York : Routledge, 2020. |
Includes bibliographical references.
Identifiers: LCCN 2019050754 (print) |
LCCN 2019050755 (ebook) | ISBN 9780367894986 (Paperback) |
ISBN 9781003019527 (eBook)
Subjects: LCSH: Inclusive education–Great Britain–Case studies.
Classification: LCC LC1203.G7 M65 2020 (print) |
LCC LC1203.G7 (ebook) | DDC 371.9/046–dc23
LC record available at https://lccn.loc.gov/2019050754
LC ebook record available at https://lccn.loc.gov/2019050755

ISBN: 978-0-367-89498-6 (pbk)
ISBN: 978-1-003-01952-7 (ebk)

Typeset in Univers
by Integra Software Services Pvt. Ltd.

Contents

Tables

Acknowledgements

Thank you to Hazel Pulley and all at Parkfield Community School and Excelsior Multi Academy Trust.

Thank you to the trustees of the No Outsiders charity and in particular Kathryn for making me do it in the first place.

Thank you to all the people who sent supportive messages to me this year.

Finally, and most importantly, thank you to my fantastic husband David. You didn't sign up for this but you're still here xx

No Outsiders is a registered charity: ref 1184725

For more information please see www.no-outsiders.com

@moffat_andrew

Preface

The Equality Act 2010

The following characteristics are protected characteristics:

Age

Disability

Gender reassignment

Marriage and civil partnership

Pregnancy and maternity

Race

Religion or belief

Sex

Sexual orientation

(legislation.gov.uk)

Ofsted guidance 2019

Personal development

- Developing responsible, respectful and active citizens who are able to play their part and become actively involved in public life as adults.

- Developing and deepening pupils' understanding of the fundamental British values of democracy, individual liberty, the rule of law, and mutual respect and tolerance.

- Promoting equality of opportunity so that all pupils can thrive together, understanding that difference is a positive, not a negative, and that individual characteristics make a person unique.

- Promoting an inclusive environment that meets the needs of all pupils, irrespective of age, disability, gender reassignment, race, religion or belief, sex or sexual orientation.

(*School Inspection Handbook*, May 2019, Gov.UK)

Chapter 1

NO OUTSIDERS IN 2020

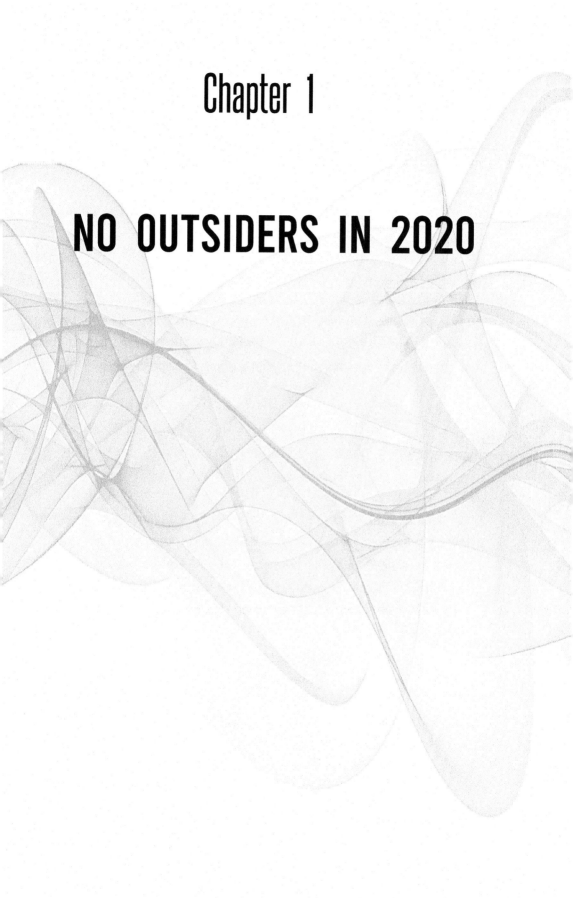

No Outsiders in 2020

In the May half-term holiday of 2019, two news articles caught my attention; one is from *Cornwalllive*, 'Brave 11-year-old speaks of racist abuse by Cornwall primary children' (Wilkinson, 2019), where a young boy speaks of the isolation he feels since his family moved from Liverpool to the south of England. During the interview the boy says,

It makes me feel kind of sad because I'm just trying to make friends. I've had loads of comments from people who don't want me there ... When I wake up in the morning it's like a burden. But it shouldn't be a chore really, it should just be going to school but every morning before going to school I feel nervous about what's going to happen there.

Three days later the BBC reported 'Children whitening skin to avoid racial hate crime, NSPCC finds' (BBC, 2019) which states figures of racial abuse and bullying of children have risen by one-fifth since 2016, with on average 29 children suffering race hate crime every day. In the article, a 10-year-old girl says,

My friends won't hang out with me anymore because people started asking why they were friends with someone who had dirty skin. I was born in the UK, but bullies tell me to go back to my own country. I don't understand because I'm from the UK ... I tried to make my face whiter before using make up so that I can fit in. I just want to enjoy going to school.

The world in 2020 presents schools with huge challenges as communities react to the disharmony around them and people retreat into 'ingroups' fearful of 'outsiders'. Educators across the UK would have been horrified to hear of the attack in a school playground in Huddersfield in 2018 on a 15-year-old refugee from Syria, filmed on the phone of a fellow pupil and later posted on social media. Following an investigation, footage emerged of the boy's sister being pulled to the ground in a separate incident as it appears pupils try to pull off her hijab (Cockburn, 2018).

These are not isolated incidents; I've taught in schools for 24 years and I have never known a climate like this for teachers and schools. Our children are not wrapped up in cotton wool; they are not immune to the messages of fear and division filtering down from voices of influence. In October 2018 the BBC reported on a rise of 40% in religious hate crimes recorded by police in the year 2017–2018 compared to the previous year. Data from the Home Office showed a record 94,098 hate incidents recorded between April 2017 and March 2018, up 17% from the previous year. Three-quarters of the incidents were classified as race related (BBC, 2018a).

We are witnessing a rise in far-right activity across Europe and America that I have not seen in my life time. Speaking to *The Observer* in October 2018, Sara Khan, Britain's first counter-extremism commissioner, described her visits to 13 cities in the UK:

> *I was really shocked that in every place I visited I heard deep concerns about the activity and impact of the far right.*
>
> *Councils across the country raised the impact the far right demonstrations have on whole towns, exploiting tensions and stoking division. I repeatedly heard about a climate of intolerance and polarisation.*
>
> (Townsend, 2018)

Writing in *The Guardian* in June 2018, Jonathan Freedland highlighted the dehumanising language used by Donald Trump when talking about migrants, which he argues echoes Nazi propaganda used 90 years previously:

> *You don't have to go back to 1930s Germany to know that the first step towards catastrophe is the dehumanisation of a reviled group. It happened that way in Rwanda and the Balkans in the 1990s, and it's happening in today's United States. 'These aren't people, they are animals,' the president said last month. They want to 'pour in to and infest our country', he tweeted this week. 'Infest' is a word reserved for rats and insects. This is language of those seeking to*

choke off human sympathy, by suggesting those suffering are not even human.

(Freedland, 2018)

What is the impact of using such language on a global scale? When people hear figures of authority using discriminatory and divisive language, is there a trickle-down effect? Professor Mary Anne Franks argues there is a real danger that others are emboldened by the behaviour: 'You have children seeing the president of the US talking like this then they will think that is the way to talk. I don't think we will see the full effect of this for decades' (Buncombe, 2018).

In my own school this year I have experienced extremely challenging reactions to the inclusion of lesbian, gay, bisexual, transgender, plus (LGBT+) equality in the No Outsiders resource. This has been well documented in the media and, at the time of writing, continues. This book is not a response to the current challenges at my school, nor is it an exploration of cause and effect; that book may come in time, once the dust has settled and I can reflect, learning lessons for the future. This resource came about simply because it is four years since I wrote *No Outsiders in Our School: Teaching the Equality Act in Primary Schools* (Moffat, 2016) and there are many newer picture books available that can be used in schools to promote the message of equality.

In the four years since the first volume of plans, No Outsiders has taken off and the response has been phenomenal. I am still working full time as Assistant Head at Parkfield school and until January 2019 the No Outsiders scheme was just one example of equality teaching in primary education. It still is in hundreds of primary settings around the UK and I spend on average one or two days out of school every week in schools delivering lessons and training staff. In the summer of 2019, No Outsiders became a registered charity. The challenges in my own school only serve to confirm how vital this work is in primary settings. After all, we know how this is going to end; it is going to end in years to come with all primary schools confidently delivering this work. We just have to get through this difficult bit.

For let us not forget the horrific consequences of not teaching about equality in primary schools: from children scared of racist bullying trying to whiten their faces in the UK to examples of children taking their own lives after homophobic bullying; 9-year-old Leia Pierce from Denver (BBC, 2018); 17-year-old Dom Sowa who endured bullying from the age of 14 when he came out on Facebook (Griffiths, 2019); Madissen Foxx Paulsen and best friend Sophia Leaf-Abrahamson, both aged 11 from North Dakota – Madissen's father believes the girls were bullied for their close relationship (Braidwood, 2019). *The Guardian* led with the headline 'Homophobic and transphobic hate crimes surge in England and Wales' (Marsh et al., 2019) on 14 June 2019 and in the same month there was widespread condemnation of the attack on a lesbian couple on a London bus resulting in charges against four teenagers, the youngest of whom was 15 years old (Osbourne, 2019).

In April 2019 Nigel Shelby, a 15-year-old student from Alabama, tragically took his own life after being bullied for his sexuality. At a school board meeting following Nigel's death, the Huntsville City Schools Superintendent was reported as saying:

> ***It's time as society to value, respect and uplift one another ... It is time for us to come together. Now is the time to teach our students and children the values of acceptance, kindness, generosity, helpfulness and just basically just being a human being.***

(Marr, 2019)

The school principal released a statement on its Facebook page: 'We were saddened this morning to learn of the death of Nigel Shelby, one of our 9th grade students. Our thoughts and prayers are with the family during this difficult time' (Marr, 2019).

Consider the response from the school and superintendent for a moment: is it enough? There is no mention of the reasons for Nigel's death and no reference to the school's response to homophobia. Indeed, the school was criticised for the lack of direct response to the homophobia that was the catalyst for this terrible event.

In 2020 we cannot sit on the fence when it comes to the teaching of equality, nor can we pick and choose which aspects of equality we feel comfortable with.

All people, regardless of race, religion, sex, gender reassignment, sexual orientation, age must feel welcome in schools with a clear ethos that spells out acceptance. Every difference needs to be included and this teaching must begin in primary schools. Children do not switch on an identity dial on their first day at secondary school; children's identities are being formed, evaluated and re-evaluated all the way through their formative years. We are all intersectional; one identity does not suffice to make up who we are. Children must be encouraged, and indeed taught, to explore identity and develop confidence in who they are as they navigate childhood and adolescence. Children must also be taught to accept the identities of others to avoid tragedies like those of Nigel, Leia, Dom, Madissen and Sophia.

In my own navigation of the challenges at my school, which I shall write about in detail elsewhere, I have had moments of doubt around the No Outsiders ethos: is it the right thing to carry on in the face of such opposition? But after months of reflection and dialogue with teachers from across the country I have reached the conclusion that there is no better time for a No Outsiders ethos. In the absence of an ethos where we teach children to identify, respect and accept their differences, what is there? What is the opposite to a No Outsiders ethos? Should we teach children that there *are* Outsiders and some people don't belong?

I am confident that the lesson plans in this volume develop the original scheme and improve the outcomes. About half of the original texts have remained. *Red Rockets and Rainbow Jelly* (Sharratt and Heap, 2003), *This Is Our House* (Rosen, 1996) and *Elmer* (Mckee, 1989) are evergreens I cannot imagine replacing; however, all lesson plans have been tweaked and updated. The lesson plan for *And Tango Makes Three* (Richardson and Parnell, 2007) is completely rewritten to reflect the responses to the book in some places around the world and consider why some books might be considered inappropriate. I have added lesson plans for 26 new texts in this resource and there is now a total of 42 books in the scheme, seven more than in the original. I highly recommend schools use Letterbox Library (www.letterboxlibrary.com) to purchase the book packs as if any books go out of print, we work together to identify a replacement and a new plan is provided in the book pack; in this way schools are never missing a book.

My advice to schools who are already using the original No Outsiders scheme is to continue with that scheme but add the new texts here in to the planning for the year. One of the aims in selecting the texts was to improve the breadth of Black, Asian and minority ethnic (BAME) characters and genders. There is no doubt in the four years since my first resource there have been huge strides forward in representation in picture books and the selection of titles here reflects that.

I am often asked where are the specific books about, for example, faith or about disability and, in answer, there are none that meet that criteria, in the same way there are no titles specifically about LGBT+ awareness. For me, the most important consideration when using a book to teach about No Outsiders is the story; I do not use issue-based books. I use books with interesting characters and stories that can then be related to issues, but the story always comes first.

There is also an aim to include references to well-being and mental health in the lesson plans for this new resource. If a child feels like an outsider, their own mental health will be adversely affected. The aim of all schools is to support well-being in their pupils and developing an ethos where children feel everyone is included will support this. The Mental Health Foundation lists the following as characteristics for good mental health:

- the ability to learn

- the ability to feel, express and manage a range of positive and negative emotions

- the ability to form and maintain good relationships with others

- the ability to cope with and manage change and uncertainty.

(Mental Health Foundation, www.mentalhealth.org.uk)

Among the stories in this resource we meet characters who overcome adversity to achieve a level of confidence and self-determination. Many characters along the way meet challenges and explore responses to negative emotions; the ability to form good reciprocal relationships with people who may have different characteristics to oneself runs like a core through the whole scheme, and stories where the management of change and a realisation that life does not often run a smooth path provide stimulus for children developing resilience in the lesson plans for older pupils. I believe good mental health is central to a No Outsiders ethos, where all children know they belong and have a valued contribution to make. That, quite simply, is the aim of the scheme.

References

BBC (2018a) 'Religious hate crimes: rise in offences recorded by police', 16 October. Available at: www.bbc.co.uk/news/uk-45874265 (accessed December 2019).

BBC (2018b) 'US boy, 9, killed himself after homophobic bullying, Mum says', 28 September. Available at: www.bbc.co.uk/news/world-us-canada-45323933 (accessed December 2019).

BBC (2019) 'Children whitening skin to avoid racial hate crime NSPCC finds', 30 May. Available at: www.bbc.co.uk/news/world-us-canada-45323933 (accessed December 2019).

Braidwood, E. (2019) 'Girls, 11, died by suicide after being bullied for questioning their sexuality', *Pink News*, 11 January.

Buncombe, A. (2018) 'Donald Trump one year on: how the Twitter President changed social media and the country's top office', *The Independent*, 17 January.

Cockburn, H. (2018) 'Sister of Syrian refugee boy assaulted in Huddersfield also attacked in video', *The Independent*, 29 November.

Freedland, J. (2018) 'Inspired by Trump, the world could be heading back to the 1930s', *The Guardian*, 22 June.

Griffiths, S. (2019) 'Stop the bullying that killed my gay son', *The Times*, 17 March.

Marr, R. (2019) 'Gay Alabama 15-year-old dies by suicide after homophobic bullying', *Metro Weekly*, 23 April.

Marsh, S., Mohdin, A. and McIntyre, N. (2019) 'Homophobic and transphobic hate crimes surge in England and Wales', *The Guardian*, 14 June.

Mckee, D. (1989) *Elmer*. London: Anderson Press.

Moffat, A. (2016) *No Outsiders in Our School: Teaching the Equality Act in Primary Schools.* Abingdon: Speechmark.

Osborne, S. (2019) 'London bus attack: teenage boys charged with homophobic attack on lesbian couple', *The Independent*, 25 July.

Richardson, J. and Parnell, P. (2007) *And Tango Makes Three.* London: Simon and Schuster.

Rosen, M. (1996) *This Is Our House.* London: Walker Books.

Sharratt, N. and Heap, S. (2003) *Red Rockets and Rainbow Jelly.* London: Penguin Books.

Townsend, M. (2018) 'UK towns polarised by rise of far right', *The Observer*, 27 October.

Wilkinson, G. (2019) 'Brave 11-year-old speaks of racist abuse by Cornwall Primary children', 27 May. Available at: www.cornwalllive.com/news/cornwall-news/brave-11-year-old-speaks-2908178 (accessed December 2019).

Chapter 2

TOLERATE, CELEBRATE, ACCEPT

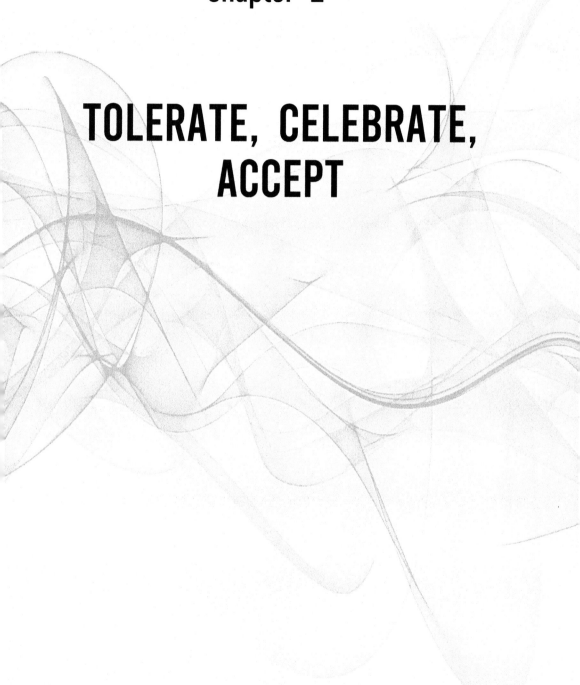

Tolerate, celebrate, accept

In the past, particularly during training sessions, I used the word 'celebrate' when defining the aims of the No Outsiders ethos. The word sounds innocuous enough; I can hear myself use it in a line such as 'We need to recognise our differences and then celebrate them'; it sounds reasonable to me. But in the last few months, the challenges around No Outsiders at my own school made me begin to question and reflect on my use of the word.

I wondered how often I used the word 'celebrate' in my original resource; I read through *No Outsiders in Our School* (Moffat, 2016) to find how often the word appeared and was surprised. I assumed the word would appear consistently as I'm aware I often use it in conversation, but I found only three examples in the introductory chapters, once on page 3 – 'we have to be delivering a curriculum that enables children to understand the benefits that exist in a society where diversity and difference are celebrated' – and again, on pages 8 and 9. However, it is the context of the second and third appearance that is key because these are part of the mission statement for the school.

The mission statement for my school in 2015 read:

> *We celebrate our rich diversity and take steps to prevent and tackle all kinds of bullying, including homophobic bullying.*
>
> *We celebrate all our children and their families without discrimination.*
>
> (Moffat, 2015, p. 9)

Until very recently I never considered not using the word 'celebrate'. The word is often used in the world of diversity and equality training as something that is a given. Surely, the argument goes, 'celebrating' each other and our differences is a good thing? It is after all much preferable to the word 'tolerate', which has overtones of 'putting up' with someone. I agree I don't want to be tolerated, I could find offence in someone saying they tolerated me, but at the same time do I really need to be 'celebrated'?

What does celebrate mean? If I celebrate you it's more than just accepting you or being your friend. If a school mission statement says we celebrate our diversity, what does that actually mean? Do we have parties every day to celebrate the fact that we have different race or religion? How do we celebrate our diversity? There is a real danger of words like 'celebrate' being tokenistic. When did I last celebrate my friend being black and what did that celebration look like? As a school we have held diversity days where children are encouraged to wear national dress and we have performances in the playground, but not every day; what happens the rest of the year? How do we celebrate the Jewish child in Year 4 or the child with a disability in Year 3?

The more I think about this, the more uncomfortable I feel about the use of the word celebrate; perhaps diversity is something that could be admired or encouraged instead. At the very least there needs to be a considered explanation of what diversity means, rather than just a bland statement about it being celebrated.

I received an email from a vicar in April 2019 which started my thinking on this. To paraphrase, while supporting the No Outsiders ethos (and indeed as a governor of a school where the ethos was embedded, he was fully supportive) the writer questioned the use of the word 'celebrate' when talking about LGBT+ equality. Even as I write this today, I can hear the roar of disapproval from defenders of LGBT+ equality, and I know the arguments: 'he wouldn't question the word celebrate when talking about race or disability, so why LGBT+? This is homophobia; it shouldn't even be a consideration'.

But I am realistic; the last six months have been a huge learning curve for me and sometimes the right thing to do is step back and listen and reflect; I am not always right. Sometimes there is no right or wrong response; there's just a response and the 'right or wrong' depends on the listener's experience and understanding. The challenge is to work with the response to find common ground while bringing people with me.

The letter encouraged me to reflect on the use of the word 'celebrate' when discussing LGBT+ equality, asking me to consider that for some people of faith, while 'tolerating' LGBT+ was realistic, 'celebrating' was not. This stuck in my throat at the time and I found it hard to step back and look at the wider picture. My initial response (though I didn't reply straight away) was to accuse this person of being homophobic and furthermore of asking me to accept his homophobia. But on reflection, was he being homophobic? The letter was full of support for No Outsiders in schools; all books were being used in the writer's own school in the year groups I recommended, and the letter offered quotes from the Bible to justify a non-judgemental approach to discussing difference. All the writer was asking for was to be allowed to tolerate rather than celebrate. Is this an unreasonable request?

I thought about this for a month or so, discussing with different people and getting a range of responses ranging from feelings of anger to feelings of frustration, or of resignation. Some responses were positive, asking: does it matter? I visited a Church of England school for a day of No Outsiders training and talked to the headteacher over lunch. His attitude was enlightening for me; he told me about his gay brother and the attitude he had towards his brother's sexuality. The headteacher told me that as a Christian he absolutely accepted and loved his brother. 'But don't ask me to go on a gay pride march,' he said.

This attitude made sense to me. I thought of my own family and the journey my parents have been on since my coming out in early 1999. It was challenging at first and together we went through some difficult times but today my parents are 100% behind me and supportive of all my No Outsiders work. I was part of Rainbow Voices, Birmingham's LGBT+ choir, for 15 years and every year they sat in the audience at concerts; they have clapped as I wrapped myself in a feather boa and stepped forward to perform a solo verse of 'I am what I am'. Recently they read No Outsiders picture books for an inclusive film and there is no question of my husband not being accepted as one of the family. But I've never asked my parents to join me on a gay pride march, and they have never offered to join me. This isn't a criticism, it's just where we are. It is important for me to celebrate Pride every year, but I don't think it is important for my parents to celebrate that with me, although they would absolutely support and accept my need to do so.

So perhaps the word to use isn't 'celebrate', or 'tolerate'; the word we should be using is 'accept'. This shift in language may not go down well with many of my LGBT+ contemporaries; there is a general acceptance in LGBT+ resources for schools that celebrating is the way forward. As I wrote in the first edition of my challenging homophobia resource back in 2007, 'Children need to understand that the world is full of different people who like different things, and we should celebrate that fact with them' (Moffat, 2007) CHIPS (Challenging Homophobia in Primary Schools) was an updated version of the 2007 resource, published by Educate and Celebrate in 2013. In CHIPS I continued the celebration narrative: 'Sessions like this cannot stand alone; they need to be part of an ethos where difference is accepted and celebrated throughout the whole school' (Moffat, 2013).

Perhaps the key is that celebrating diversity as a concept is not the same as celebrating the individual characteristics. We can celebrate the reality of a diverse community without celebrating the individual unique characteristics of that diversity. Rather than saying we respect different opinions, we are saying we respect the right to have differences of opinions. I may not agree with your opinion, I may not respect your opinion, but I respect the right for you to hold that opinion.

Valuing All God's Children (Church of England, 2019) is a guide for CofE schools on challenging homophobic bullying and is a useful tool to use when looking at this area from a perspective of faith. The vision for education states: 'Pupils are helped to work out how to live fulfilled, embodied lives; how to be happy with the skin they are in. They are also encouraged to celebrate the wonderful variety of different ways of being human' (p. 10).

The guide reinforces this statement with a quote from Genesis 1:27: 'All are made in the image of God and are loved by God. Through the example of Jesus all are called to live embodied, fulfilled human lives' (p. 10).

The guide continues:

> ***In any Church of England school classroom, it is likely that not all will agree on issues to do with human sexuality, marriage and gender identity. However, there needs to be a faithful and loving commitment to remain in relationship with the other and honour the***

> *dignity of their humanity without 'back turning', dismissing the other*
> *person, or claiming superiority.*
>
> (p. 11)

I like the wording used in this guidance; to celebrate 'the variety of different ways we are human' is different from celebrating individual unique characteristics such as disability or LGBT+ or race. The key is that we are celebrating *being* different, rather than celebrating *the* differences. In the context of teaching about LGBT+ equality, if a person finds tension in celebrating different sexual orientation, can that person accept sexual orientation as something that just exists? Schools can celebrate our rich diversity; it's the diversity itself that is celebrated rather than the individual characteristics. Those individual characteristics are something that are accepted in the context of our diverse communities to ensure no one is pushed out or excluded.

Following a paragraph where the diversity of sexual orientation that exists in schools is acknowledged as 'the lived reality of educational contexts in modern England', the advice is:

> *Schools need to support pupils who are members of a minority*
> *group or who are perceived to be different: these pupils are*
> *vulnerable to being bullied and to being made to feel like outsiders*
> *and unwelcome. We need to ensure that no child or young person*
> *can leave a Church of England School without a sense of their own*
> *belovedness and without being offered honour as a person of divine*
> *indwelling.*
>
> (p. 12)

Note the absence of the word celebrate in that paragraph, but the inclusion of many phrases that stir feelings of togetherness and self-worth. I am not a person of faith, but I want children to have a sense of their own 'belovedness'; who doesn't want to feel they are loved, accepted, that their indwelling, whatever its source, is honoured?

There is similar supportive advice to Orthodox Jewish Schools in their duty to safeguard LGBT+ pupils in their care (Mirvis, 2018):

Orthodox schools have understandably found it difficult to engage with LGBT+ issues. As challenging as the task might be, and it is exceptionally challenging, I believe that failure to address it all amounts to an obrogation of our responsibility to the almighty and to our children.

(p. 3)

The guide continues:

when homophobic, biphobic and transphobic bullying is carried out with 'justifications' from Jewish texts, a major chilul Hashem (desecration of God's name) is caused. We must be ever mindful of the mitzva to 'love your neighbour as yourself' (Vayikra/Leviticus 19:18), considered by Rabbi Akiva to be the most important principle of the Torah.

(p. 3)

Concluding his introduction, Mirvis argues for a whole school approach to the well-being of LGBT+ young people: 'This requires robust behaviour policies alongside wider school work to integrate understanding and awareness about LGBT+ experiences' (p. 4).

Again, the word celebrate is absent, but these guides are illuminating in the way they respectfully traverse the complicated road towards full LGBT+ equality within the faith context. There is no lack of commitment to the goal of equality we share, but there is also acknowledgement that to throw the word 'celebrate' around is misguided. We're not all on the same page; our lived experiences and understandings have brought us to where we are today and we hold our ideas, and ideas can change, but we have different starting points.

I have done much soul searching on this use of language and I remain open to discussion and debate around the way forward; I reserve the right to change my mind in the future as I have done in the past. But for now, my experience informs me to use less of the word 'celebrate' and more of the word 'accept' when teaching about LGBT+ equality. I will teach children to explore and celebrate their own identities (note the plural – our intersectionality allows us to hold more than one identity) while accepting the parts of others that make their identities. I want all children, including LGBT+ children, to explore who they are and know they belong in my class, and this means talking about LGBT+ identity alongside other identities. Meanwhile I am very happy to be gay myself, and I'm celebrating that every day; I don't expect you to celebrate my sexual orientation with me, however I do expect it to be accepted without judgement in the same way I will accept the parts of you that may be different to me.

There is no headlining shift in the ethos of No Outsiders; the central theme remains: everyone different, everyone welcome, no one is an outsider. However, my hope is that I am demonstrating respect and consideration for those who have different beliefs to me. I am confident the aims of the resource remain strong, and provide an ethos which every school, every person can sign up to.

References

Church of England (2019) *Valuing All God's Children: Guidance for Church of England Schools on Challenging Homophobic, Biphobic and Transphobic Bullying.* Available at: www.churchofengland.org/sites/default/files/2019-07/Valuing%20All%20God%27s%20Children%20July%202019_0.pdf (accessed December 2019).

Mirvis, E. (2018) *The Wellbeing of LGBT+ Pupils: A Guide for Orthodox Jewish Schools.* Available at: https://chiefrabbi.org/wp-content/uploads/2018/09/The-Wellbeing-of-LGBT-Pupils-A-Guide-for-Orthodox-Jewish-Schools.pdf (accessed December 2019).

Moffat, A. (2007) *Challenging Homophobia In Primary Schools: An Early Years Resource.* Birmingham: Birmingham City Council.

Moffat, A. (2013) CHIPS: Challenging Homophobia in Primary Schools, Educate and Celebrate. (No longer available.).

Moffat, A. (2016) *No Outsiders in Our School: Teaching the Equality Act in Primary Schools.* Abingdon: Speechmark.

Chapter 3

SO MUCH GOOD IN THE WORLD

No Outsiders assemblies

So much good in the world

The books and lesson plans in the No Outsiders resource are not enough to embed the ethos; there are seven lesson plans for each year group which works out at one per half term plus an extra. There are brilliant new picture books coming out all the time and www.no-outsiders.com provides extra lesson plans based on new books not included in this scheme, updated throughout the year. But pressures on the tight curriculum mean a weekly No Outsiders lesson may be unrealistic so we need to find other ways to talk about equality in the everyday mechanisms of school.

No Outsiders assemblies ensure children are hearing a message of equality at least once a week. In my own school I deliver these assemblies to year groups once a week and I know some secondary schools use these plans as tutor group sessions. They can be used as personal development starters or as discussion pieces at the start/end of the day. I don't recommend these images are used for whole school assemblies; there are many I would not use in Key Stage 1 and also the discussions I have with children in Year 3 are different to those I have with Year 6 children.

For the most part I use these assembly pictures with Key Stage 2. I'm not going to list here which I would use with Key Stage 1; teachers know their children and don't need me to be prescriptive. Often in Key Stage 1 assemblies I lead with an image of a child being left out (different image each week) and ask children to tell me what is happening:

- What is happening here?

- How is the child feeling? (Like an outsider)

- What does the child need to hear?

- What could you say to the children who are leaving the child out?

- If you saw this on our playground what would you do?

- What line could you say to the child? ('Come and play with me'; 'Are you ok?'; 'Do you want to be my friend?'; 'I'll be your friend')

- How can we make sure this doesn't happen at our school?

Then I show a picture of (diverse) children smiling and playing together and I say this picture reminds me much more of our school; why is that?

- What do you notice about the children? (They are different)

- How are they different? (Skin, hair, eyes, gender, wheelchair etc)

- Are they friends? How do you know? (They are smiling and playing)

- Is anyone in this picture feeling like an outsider? How do you know?

- Which of the two pictures is more like our school? Why?

There are hundreds of suitable pictures available on the web that we can use to contrast in this way and for most Key Stage 1 No Outsiders assemblies this is what I use, occasionally using a Key Stage 2 assembly picture when I feel the story is accessible. We also use the No Outsiders assembly to announce our celebration awards for the week; behaviour, house points, maths awards etc. The assemblies last no longer than 15 minutes.

Assembly pictures and plans can be found on the No Outsiders website (www.no-outsiders.com) and are freely available. There is an archive of over 300 as I post at least one a week and schools across the UK use them, often copying me into tweets about responses to them. Children often talk to me about the assembly pictures during the week and they are disappointed if for some reason a week is missed.

Children enjoy finding out about the world around them, and the purpose of the stories is to promote a sense of belonging and community cohesion in the child. Children taking part in these assemblies will leave feeling confident and happy about positive events happening around the world. I am not denying bad things happen, but I am focusing on good things: 'Look at this,' I am saying; 'Isn't this wonderful! You see, people around the world agree with us and our No Outsiders school!'

Below is a list of 20 No Outsiders pictures and plans. Also included is the link to the original story. My aim is to show the breadth of No Outsiders images that can be used across the year and schools may choose to use these images throughout the year, but I do recommend people explore the website or my Twitter feed @moffat_andrew each week for the most up-to-date pictures and plans as there are new ones every week that often link to current news stories that children may have heard about. It was difficult to pick 20 pictures from a list of 300; my aim was to show a range of topics. For each assembly I have included a link to the original news story and where possible referenced the journalist.

Week 1: Back to school

We want to start to start the new year off by modelling to children the behaviour we expect and this picture says it all. A smiling little boy proudly wears a shirt with the words, 'I will be your friend'. Blake was asked by his Mum to choose a design for a shirt to wear on his first day at school and rather than a dinosaur, dragon or sports team, he asked for these words. The photo went viral with people using #blakesfriends. Blake wants to make sure no one feels like an outsider at his school; he will be their friend.

- What is the first day back at school like?

- What different feelings do children have when they start school?

- Why do you think Blake chose to wear this shirt?

- Why doesn't Blake's shirt say, 'I will be your friend if you are black' or 'I will be your friend if you are white' or 'I will be your friend if you are Christian'?

- Does Blake care about the race or religion of his friends? Do you think Blake cares if his friends have disabilities, different genders or different families?

- What kind of person do you think Blake is?

- Do you think Blake will have lots of friends? Why?

- Why are people wearing shirts with the message #blakesfriends?

- What can we learn from Blake?

- Why is this story about No Outsiders?

(Annie Reneau, 2019)

Week 2: Friendship

The photo shows Kamden and Paul who are best friends; they both love superheroes and meet up to watch videos. Kamden uses a wheelchair and one day Paul was horrified when he saw his friend's chair tip up and Kamden fall out. The problem was Kamden had grown too big for his chair, but his family could not afford to buy a new one. Paul said, 'His wheelchair has fallen forward so many times and that sucks. Also he has a really hard time pushing it because it's so heavy.'

Paul decided he needed to help his friend so he investigated ways to raise money. Paul asked his Mum to set up a Go Fund Me page to raise $3900 for a new chair. In 26 days the page had raised $5935.

Kamden's mum said, 'What really contributes to their friendship is that Paul does not see Kamden as someone who has a disability. He sees him as Kamden. Because of that, Kamden truly is himself around him.' Paul never acted as though his friend was different.

- Why did Kamden fall out of his wheelchair?

- What do you think Paul did when his friend fell out of his wheelchair? What do you think Paul said to Kamden?

- Why do you think the fundraiser raised so much money so quickly?

- Where did that money come from?

- What does that tell us about people around the world today and attitudes toward disability?

- Kamden's mum says, 'Paul does not see Kamden as someone who has a disability' – what does she mean?

- Who could have been an outsider in this story?

- What happened to make sure that person was not an outsider?

- What can we learn from Kamden and Paul?

- Why is this story about No Outsiders?

(Avery Friedman, 2017)

Week 3: Viking warrior

The photo shows a Viking helmet. Over 100 years ago a Viking grave was discovered in Birka, Sweden. Along with the body in the grave were a sword and shield, a spear and axe, arrows, two horses and a strategy board showing the person was a military leader who planned battles. The grave has been called 'the ultimate warrior Viking grave' by historians.

Historian Anna Kjellstrom from Stockholm University was studying the bones for another project and noticed the bones resembled those of a female. DNA tests were carried out and the conclusion was that the Viking warrior was female. This discovery made news headlines across the world.

- What is your image of a Viking warrior?

- Why did everyone always think this warrior was a man?

- What does this show about the way we often see male and female roles?

- What is a gender stereotype?

- Anna the historian wrote, 'the biological sex was taken for granted' – what does she mean?

- How is this story an example of a gender stereotype?

- What does this story show about how some women were treated in Viking times?

- What does this story show about ideas about history? (ideas can change)

- What can we learn from Anna Kjellstrom?

- What can we learn from this Viking warrior?

- Why is this story about No Outsiders?

(Louise Nordstrom, 2017)

Week 4: Jack and Rani

Jack and Rani from a school in Manchester have become famous in the UK because of their friendship and the way they met. Rani is a refugee from Iraq and was bullied in his first few days at school until Jack met him and they became friends.

Jack said, 'He was in a corner by himself so I thought, "he needs a friend". So I thought I'll go up to him and ask him, "How are you? Where are you from?"'

'He said Syria and I took a step back because on the TV, on the radio you hear bad things about it. But then I said, "come and join us, come and join our group", and he did and here we are.'

Jack and Rani appeared on the Channel 4 programme *Educating Greater Manchester* and since then have been on *This Morning* to talk about their friendship. They have received a huge amount of praise on Twitter and social media; one tweet said, 'The whole world could learn something from Jack.'

- What do Jack and Rani have in common?

- What are their differences?

- Why was Rani alone?

- Why do you think Jack approached Rani and said, 'How are you'?

- Why did Jack take a step back when Rani said he was from Syria?

- Jack could have walked away at that point but he stayed; what was the impact of his actions?

- Jack and Rani became famous because of their story; why?

- What does this show about people in the UK today?

- Why are people saying every school needs a Jack? What do they mean?

- What can we learn from Jack?

- Why is this story about No Outsiders?

(Rachel Hosie, 2017)

Week 5: We dine together

The image shows an older child shaking hands with a younger child who appears to be sitting alone. A high school in Florida, USA, has set up a lunchtime club to make sure no one sits alone to eat. 'We dine together' aims to make sure every student has someone to share their lunch break with. Students in the club roam the high school at lunch time and if they see someone alone, they approach and introduce themselves.

Denis Estimon came to the US from Haiti as a child and remembers feeling alone as he started school. He says, 'If we don't try and go make that change, who's going to do it?' Denis set up the club with his friends. Denis added, 'It's not a good feeling, you're by yourself. And that's something I don't want anybody to go through.'

- Denis could just sit with his own friends at lunch. Why do you think he chose to set up the club?

- Why do some children sit alone?

- How do you think a student feels when approached by the We Dine Together Club?

- What do you think is the impact on the school?

- Could we do that at our school?

- What can we learn from Denis?

- Why is this story about No Outsiders?

(Taylor Pittman, 2017)

Week 6: Finish line

Ten-year-old Riley was 60m from the finish line of a cross country race in Grimsby when he collapsed with a stitch. Another runner, Julian, picked up Riley and carried him across the finish line. Local photographer Jon Corken captured the moment perfectly.

Later, Julian said, 'I'd rather not have won and helped my friend than leave him there.'

The headteacher of Julian's school said, 'What Julian did encompasses how we want our children to be. He has exemplified his caring attitude. He is one of our young leaders where he helps support younger children within the school with extra classes. I am proud to say we have a school full of Julians.'

- What's happening in the picture?

- How do you think Riley felt when he collapsed?

- What were the choices facing Julian as he ran past Riley?

- Why did Julian choose to stop and help Riley?

- How do you think Riley felt when Julian stopped for him?

- In what ways are the boys similar?
  In what ways are the boys different?
  Does the picture suggest either child is bothered about race?

- What are the words on Julian's shirt? What do you think they mean?

- What can we learn from Julian?

- What does Julian's headteacher mean when she says, 'We have a school full of Julians'?

- Why is this story about No Outsiders?

(BBC, 2017a)

Week 7: Dialogue breaking down prejudice

Beverley sat down on a plane next to Jiva and watched her write a text to someone in Arabic including the word Allah. Beverley panicked and raised concerns with a steward but the steward told Beverley if she had an issue, she could leave the plane instead of Jiva.

Jiva and Beverley then sat together for the plane journey and talked. Jiva explained that Allah meant God in Arabic; she was texting a friend to give her support after her car was broken in to and wrote, 'HasbiAllahu la ilaaha illaahu alayhi tawakaltu/may Allah make the day easy for you.'

Once the pair started talking, Jiva said she could tell Beverley was remorseful; Beverley said, 'It's so scary what the media can make us just think.' By the end of the flight Beverley and Jiva were friends and have since kept in touch.

- Why did Beverley panic? (She didn't understand Arabic, perhaps she has never talked to someone who is Muslim.)

- What was Jiva's response?

- Jiva could have shouted 'How dare you!' at Beverley and not talked to her. Why do you think Jiva chose to talk to Beverley instead?

- How do you think Beverley felt as Jiva talked to her?

- How did Beverley and Jiva become friends?

- What did Beverley learn from this experience?

- What can we learn from this story?

- Why is this story about No Outsiders?

(Wayne Ankers, 2016)

Week 8: Boys shall go to the ball

Disney has apologised for not allowing a boy to join their 'Princess for a day' experience. When the boy's mother tried to book the day for her son Noah, she was told he would not be allowed to take part because he was a boy. Her son was offered a cuddly toy instead.

Noah is a *Frozen* super-fan and loves to dress up as Elsa. Noah's mum wrote an open letter asking 'What terrible, awful fate may befall' her son if he wears a dress. Disney apologised, saying the experience was open to all children aged 3 to 12.

Noah's mother said, 'If a little girl wants to be a superhero, she can be. If she wants to be a Jedi, she can be. She can be whatever she wants.'

After apologising, Disney released a statement:

> *Diversity is near and dear to our hearts and we want to make sure that all our guests enjoy their experience at our resort. Of course, both boys and girls are welcome to enjoy the Princess for a Day experience in addition to all our other special activities.*

Noah's story hit news headlines around the world and his mum received huge support on social media following the incident. Writing after the incident, Noah's mum said 'Now Noah, and every other little boy who wants to, SHALL go to the ball!'

The wording on the Disneyland Paris website used to read: 'Grant every little girl's wishes with a Princess experience'. The website has been changed and now reads 'Grant every child's wishes with a Princess experience'.

- Why did Noah's mum feel so angry?

- Why did his mum ask, 'What terrible, awful fate may befall my son if he wears a dress'? What was she trying to show?

- Why did Disney apologise? Why didn't Disney continue to say boys could not join the experience?

- Why have Disney said, 'Diversity is near and dear to our hearts'?

- Why have Disney changed the wording on their website?

- What does this show about Disney and the world today?

- What law in the UK says that you should not face discrimination because of your gender? (The Equality Act 2010)

- Who was facing discrimination in this story?

- What can we learn from Noah's mum?

- What can we learn from Disney?

- Why is this story about No Outsiders?

(Kevin Rawlinson, 2017; Jimmy Nsubuga, 2017)

Week 9: Food diversity

The photo shows a supermarket in Hamburg with empty shelves. The shop emptied shelves of all foreign-made produce to help people think about racism.

Shoppers at Edeka store were able to see how many goods were made outside of Germany, and many shelves were empty. The shop put up signs saying, 'This shelf is pretty boring without diversity.'

A spokesperson from Edeka said,

> *Edeka stands for variety and diversity. In our stores we sell numerous foods which are produced in the various regions of Germany. But only*

together with products from other countries is it possible to create the unique variety that our customers value.

- Why do you think Edeka did this?

- What did this show their shoppers?

- What does the sign about the boring shelf mean?

- Where does the food that we buy come from? Does it all come from England?

- Why don't shops in England sell only food that is made in England, and shops in Germany sell only food that was is made in Germany?

- What does this demonstrate about different people around the world and how we live together?

- Some people think that if we have different skin or live in different places or have different faith, that we can't get along. What do we say in our school?

- What can we learn from Edeka?

- Why is this story about No Outsiders?

(Will Worley, 2017)

Week 10: Men holding hands

The first photo shows two men holding hands. The story explains men all over the Netherlands are holding hands to protest against homophobia following an attack on two gay men in Amsterdam. The men told police the attack started because they were holding hands. Following the attack, a peaceful march was held through Amsterdam attended by hundreds of people, holding hands to show support.

Journalist Barbara Barend then tweeted a call for 'all men (straight and gay) please to just walk hand in hand' and a trend started under

#allemannenhandinhand where men from across the world flooded Twitter and Instagram with holding hands photos. They included footballers, boxers, soldiers and two politicians arriving at a meeting at the Dutch parliament holding hands.

The men in the final photo work in Utrecht hospital in Amsterdam and the translation of their tweet is 'Because love and care is for everyone'.

- Why did Barbara Barend call for all men to walk hand in hand?

- Why did she say 'straight and gay'? Why not just gay men?

- Why do you think there are so many photos from around the world?

- What does this show about people around the world?

- Why have politicians joined in?

- What do the people in the photo write 'Love and care is for everyone'?

- How do you think the people who were attacked feel about the response?

- Why is this story about No Outsiders?

- Why do some people attack people who are different? (Because they don't understand about diversity and equality and no outsiders.)

- What can you do if you meet someone who doesn't understand about No Outsiders?

(*The Guardian*, 2017; BBC 2017b)

Week 11: People can change

The photo shows a man having tattoos removed. A tattoo shop owner in Maryland, USA, is removing racist tattoos for free. The aim for Southside Tattoo is to help people who have changed their minds about the way they live their lives. The shop also removes gang related tattoos.

Shop owner Dave Cutlip calls his service 'random acts of tattoo'. He says, 'Sometimes people make bad choices and sometimes people change. We believe there is enough hate in the world and we want to make a difference.'

Where tattoos are big sometimes Dave can't remove them but he will cover them up with different art. A man came into his shop with 'White' on one arm and 'Power' on the other, a result of a year spent in prison. Dave covered up the 'White' with a heart and two roses and 'Power' with an eagle.

Dave has set up a crowdfunding page on Facebook to raise money for other tattoo shops to do the same.

- Why do some people have tattoos?

- Not all tattoos are words, some are pictures or patterns that mean something to that person. Why would someone have a racist tattoo made?

- If someone had a racist tattoo five years ago, why might they want it removed now?

- Some people in the story say they want racist tattoos removed because people judge them and they can't get jobs. What does that show about people where they live?

- How do people change their minds?

- How is Dave changing lives?

- What can we learn from the people having racist tattoos covered up?

- What can we learn from Dave?

- Why is this story about No Outsiders? (Because it shows people can change their minds. Someone who is used to be racist may not always be racist.)

(Justin W.M. Moyer, 2017)

Week 12: Autism poem

The photo shows Benjamin Giroux writing a poem. He is 10 years old and for homework he decided to write a poem called 'I am' about how it feels for him to live with autism.

Benjamin's poem explains how he feels different. The poem has gone viral and the National Autistic Society has shared it.

- What is autism (I asked a child with autism how to describe what autism means. Oliver told me, 'Autism is your brain wired differently so you see the world in a different way. It's just a different view of the world.' Oliver says some things are harder for him but also he is better at some things than other children.)

- Benjamin said he didn't want to write a poem that just rhymed, why do you think he chose to write this poem?

- Why does Benjamin say, 'I'm odd ... I wonder if you are too? (Is he saying that we are all different; we all have things about us that are 'odd'?)

- Why does Benjamin say, 'I feel like a boy in outer space, I touch the stars and feel out of place'?

- How does Benjamin feel when people laugh at him? He says it makes him 'shrink' – what does he mean?

- What does 'castaway' mean? Why does Benjamin choose to use that word?

- Benjamin says 'I dream of a day that it's ok, I try to fit in, I hope that some day I do' – what does Benjamin want more than anything else?

- This poem has gone viral; why do you think that is? What does this show about how people around the world feel about autism and people being different?

- How can we help Benjamin?

- What can we do in our school today to make sure no one feels like a castaway?

- If you could meet Benjamin what would you say to him?

- Why is this story about No Outsiders?

(Ilona Baliūnaitė, 2019)

Week 13: Houses of Parliament Pride

The photo shows the Houses of Parliament lit up in the colours of the rainbow flag to celebrate London Pride in 2017. This was the first time this had happened.

The year 2017 marked 50 years since homosexuality was decriminalised in the UK. In 1972 the first gay pride was held in London, with 2000 people taking part. This year 26,000 people joined the parade to celebrate LGBT+ equality and 1 million people lined the streets to watch and cheer to show their support.

- Who works in the Houses of Parliament?

- What is the building for?

- What/who is the rainbow flag for?

- What is London Pride about?

- Why do you think the MPs decided to light up the building in the rainbow flag on the day of London Pride?

- Fifty years ago it was against the law to be LGBT+. What does this picture demonstrate about ideas? (It shows that ideas can change and people can change.)

- What law in the UK protects LGBT+ people from discrimination? (The Equality Act 2010)

- Who else is protected in the Equality Act 2010?

- Why is this photo about No Outsiders?

(Pride in London, 2017)

Week 14: Olympic ski story

The cross country skiing event at the Winter Olympics 2018 was won by Dario Cologna of Switzerland but the race became famous for the people who came in last, 23 minutes later.

Finishing in 114th place, 3rd from last, seen here in the picture, was Pita Taufatofua from Tongo, who had never seen snow a year ago. Pita practised on roller skis and his first time on snow was only 12 weeks ago. Pita said his aim in the event was to finish before the lights went out and avoid skiing into a tree.

Pita then waited at the finish line with other competitors from Colombia, Morocco and Portugal for the person who came in last: German Madrasgo from Mexico who came 116th. As German crossed the line he was greeted with huge cheers and was hoisted up on the shoulders of his competitors while he waved his flag. German only started skiing last year. This picture quickly went viral around the world.

As he was interviewed later, Pita Taufatofua said, 'I'd rather be finishing towards the end of the pack with all my friends than in the middle by myself. We fought together, we finished together.'

- Why are they smiling and cheering?

- The man on their shoulders came last; why is he celebrating?

- Why did Pita and other competitors wait for German?

- The three men in the picture are all different nationalities and may have different language, faith, culture; what does this demonstrate about different people? (We have things that unite us.)

- Why did the picture go viral?

- Why didn't a picture of the person who won the race go viral? What does this show about people around the world?

- What can we learn from Pita and German?

- Why is this story about No Outsiders?

(Tyler Lauletta, 2018)

Week 15: Archery and difference

Faith Oakley is a world class archer; she is ranked in the top 10 high school archers in the world.

Faith started archery as a young child at a summer camp where her teacher suggested she join in the sport. Faith thought she could not take part because she is unable to use her right arm: 'I told her she was crazy; I didn't have enough hands.'

But her teacher held the bow and Faith pulled back the string with her other arm. Faith loved the sport and then started using her teeth to pull back the string instead of her arm:

> *I put the arrow on my string and hold it in my teeth, then I take a deep breath. I inhale and exhale a couple of times, then pull the string back and hold it at my aim point for two seconds and then I let go with my mouth.*

A coach at Faith's team says: 'She aims differently, stands differently. Everything is different. But she never wants to be treated differently and she's extremely determined and dedicated.'

Faith says, 'Instead of tearing myself down, I'm working hard on making myself learn from my mistakes. I don't get down on myself, I think about how I'm going to fix this and reapply myself and do it better next time.'

- How do we see most archers use their equipment?

- What is different about Faith?

- Why do you think at summer camp Faith's teacher suggested she have a go at archery when she knew Faith's arm worked differently?

- What was the impact of the teacher finding a way to get Faith involved?

- What does this demonstrate about attitudes towards differences in people and disabilities?

- Faith's coach says 'Everything is different' about the way Faith takes part in the sport. What does this demonstrate about her team?

- Faith says, 'I think about how I'm going to fix this and reapply myself.' Can she 'fix' her arm? What does she mean by this?

- What can we learn from Faith?

- Why is this story about No Outsiders?

(Kirby Adams, 2017)

Week 16: North Pole

Eleven women from Europe and the Middle East have become famous for trekking to the North Pole together. The women aged 28–50 are from Qatar, Sweden, Iceland, Omar, Russia, France, Saudi Arabia, Cyprus, Kuwait, Slovenia and the UK.

The project was set up by Felicity Aston, with two aims: scientific discovery and also to foster good relations between European and Arabian women. Ida Olssen from Sweden said even before they started, she'd gained a new understanding of why some women wear head coverings:

In my mind it always felt forced – that men forced the women to do it. But when the girls here talk about it, it's something they actually want to do; they're not forced to do it. That was completely new to me.

Ida also said she wanted to show women and girls that you didn't need to be a superhero to achieve a big objective. The group trekked together through temperatures of -36 degrees pulling heavy sledges. Those who were better at skiing would go on ahead and then waited for the others to catch up so the group stayed together.

Before this trip there were no records of female travellers in the North Pole. The final photo shows the group at the moment they reached the North Pole. Everyone held a flag for the photo.

- Why do you think until now there are only records of men travelling to the North Pole?

- Why do you think Felicity Aston set up the expedition?

- Why do you think Felicity chose to involve women from so many different backgrounds? What was she trying to show?

- How did Ida learn about women wearing head coverings? (She asked questions.)

- Today in the UK, what is the best way to learn about different people and different cultures? (Talk to people and ask questions.)

- Why is the UK a great place to find out about different people? (Because it is diverse.)

- Some of the group were better skiers than others. Why didn't they ski faster to get to the North Pole first?

- Why did the explorers hold flags for the photo? What were they showing?

- Why is this story about No Outsiders? (If a child says it's not about No Outsiders because there are no men, say that's an interesting point – what do we think? Why did Felicity choose to just have women this time; what has happened in the past? What is she trying to show about women today? It is about No Outsiders because in the past women have been left out. Also because Felicity is making sure people from different countries work together. In future how can explorers make sure all expeditions are inclusive?)

(Elizabeth Renstrom, 2018)

Week 17: Different families

As Todd Bachman walked his daughter Brittany down the aisle at the start of her wedding, he stopped the procession. He ran to the front row and grabbed the hand of Brittany's step-dad, taking him to walk their daughter down the aisle together.

Later in an interview the step-dad said, 'He came and grabbed my hand and said, "You worked as hard as I have. You'll help us walk our daughter down the aisle" … I got weak in my knees and lost it. Nothing better in my life, the most impactful moment in my life.'

The two dads admitted they had not always got along, but Todd said, 'For me to thank him for all the years of helping raise our daughter wouldn't be enough. There is no better way to thank somebody than to assist me walking her down the aisle.'

- What is a wedding for?

- What is 'walking down the aisle'? Traditionally who does that bit?

- Why has Brittany got two dads?

- Why do you think Brittany's step-dad wasn't asked to walk her down the aisle?

- How do you think he felt as he watched Todd walk Brittany down the aisle?

- Why did Todd stop the procession?

- Look at the face of the guest next to the step-dad as Todd grabs his hand; what is she thinking?

- Look at Todd's face; what is he thinking?

- How is the step-dad feeling?

- How do you think Brittany felt when she saw both her dads walking down the aisle together?

- Why is this about different families?

- Why have the photos gone viral? What does this show us about how people across the world see families?

- What can we learn from Todd?

- Why is this about No Outsiders?

(Brittany Wong, 2019)

Week 18: World leaders photo

At the NATO summit in Brussels last week the partners of world leaders gathered for a photo. The group included Gautier Destenay, who is husband of the Prime Minister of Luxembourg, Xavier Battel. The Prime Minister of Luxembourg is the only openly gay world leader.

The photo was celebrated across the world as a symbol of LGBT+ equality.

When the White House published the photo on their official Facebook page, each of the partners was named apart from Gautier, whose name was missing from the list. Gautier's name was added to the list later.

- Why is this photo important?

- What does this photo show us about attitudes towards gay people today?

- When Gautier's name was missed off the list of people it could have been a mistake, but what is the consequence of that mistake? What does it look like?

- Why do you think the list was later changed to include Gautier's name?

- If there is only one openly gay world leader and all the other partners in the photo are women, what else does this photo show us about world leaders? (They are all men.)

- What can we learn from this photo?

- Why is this photo about No Outsiders? Is it about No Outsiders?

(Martin Pengelly, 2017)

Week 19: Racist graffiti

Gregory Locke from NYC boarded a subway train at Manhattan to find swastikas and racist graffiti daubed on all of the advertisements. He wrote on Facebook, 'The train was silent as everyone stared at each other, uncomfortable and not sure what to do.' Gregory went on to say:

> *One guy got up and said, 'Hand sanitiser gets rid of sharpie. We need alcohol.' He found some tissues and got to work. I've never seen so many people simultaneously reach into their bags and pockets looking for tissues and Purel. Within about 2 minutes all the Nazi symbolism was gone.*

Later, Gregory said, 'Seeing a bunch of strangers stand up for, and come together to stand up for what everyone knows is right, was very heartening.'

- Where does racist graffiti come from?

- Why do some people write racist graffiti? (Because they don't understand about equality and diversity – and no one has convinced them about No Outsiders.)

- Why do you think people on the subway train were silent and uncomfortable?

- When one man started cleaning off the graffiti, what happened? Why do you think everyone joined in?

- The people could have chosen to ignore the graffiti. Why do you think they chose not to ignore it?

- What were the consequences of their actions?

- How do you think people felt when they left the train having cleaned it off?

- What does this show us about lots of people in NYC and what they think about racism?

- What can we learn from the people in this story?

- Why is this story about No Outsiders?

(Nina Golgowski, 2017)

Week 20: Manchester vigil

Thousands of people attended a vigil last night in Manchester to remember the victims of the tragic events on Monday night and show the city can work together. Young people from different faith and community groups were joined by the Lord Mayor who said the thoughts of the whole city were with those affected.

The Bishop of Manchester said, 'We are Manchester'.

One member of the crowd, Hani Singh, said, 'I came out tonight to show we are not afraid. So many people tonight have come from so many different communities and it shows we are united against terrorism.'

Poet Tony Walsh read out an ode to Manchester which included the lines:

We make you feel welcome and we make summat happen
And we can't seem to help it

And if you're looking from history, then yeah we've a wealth

But the Manchester way is to make it yourself.

- Who came to the vigil?

- Were there people of different faith and culture at the vigil? People with disabilities, people who are LGBT+, different ethnicities, genders and ages? What does this show us about Manchester?

- What does the Bishop mean when he says 'We are Manchester'?

- What does the poet mean when he says, 'If you're looking from history then yeah we've a wealth'?

- What can we learn from Manchester and this vigil?

- Why is this story about No Outsiders?

(Chris Slater, 2017)

References

Adams, K. (2017) 'With the use of only one arm, Faith Oakley is determined to be one of the best archers in the world', *Courier Journal*, 21 November. Available at: www.courier-journal.com/story/life/wellness/fitness/2017/11/21/kentuckyteen-world-champion-archer/846040001/

Ankers, W. (2016) 'Passenger refuses to sit beside Muslim who she saw texting word Allah – but they end becoming friends', *Mirror*, 21 July. Available at: www.mirror.co.uk/news/uk-news/passenger-refuses-sit-beside-muslim-8464738?ICID=FB_mirror_main

Baliūnaitė, I. (2019) 'Autistic Boy Writes Moving Poem About How Odd He Is For A School Assignment, Leaves Teacher In Tears', *boredpanda*. Available at: https://www.boredpanda.com/autistic-student-poem-being-odd-benjamin-giroux/?utm_source=google&utm_medium=organic&utm_campaign=organic (accessed February 2020).

BBC (2017a) '"Brownlee moment" as pupil carries friend to finishing line', 9 March. Available at: https://www.bbc.co.uk/news/uk-england-humber-39215616 (accessed February 2020).

BBC (2017b) 'Dutch men hold hands to protest against homophobia', 5 April. Available at: https://www.bbc.co.uk/news/world-europe-39505692 (accessed February 2020).

Friedman, A. (2017) 'This eight year old raised almost $6000 to buy his best friend a new wheelchair', *Global Citizen*, 27 July. Available at: www.globalcitizen.org/en/content/boy-

buys-new-wheelchair-best-friend/?fbclid=IwAR39tB1271LflXXGfRMscqlaVYWc4WcLNaRVX
ujNywE55r9i1RidjQcCjgw

Golgowski, N. (2017) 'Subway riders rise up to clean swastikas from New York train', *Huffpost*, 6 February. Available at: www.huffingtonpost.com/entry/subway-riders-clean-swastikas_us_589728a8e4b0c1284f265adb

Guardian, The (2017) 'Dutch men walk hand in hand for solidarity after gay couple attacked', 6 April. Available at: https://www.theguardian.com/world/2017/apr/06/dutch-men-hand-in-hand-solidarity-gay-couple-attacked (accessed February 2020).

Hosie, R (2017) 'Video of schoolboy who befriended Syrian refugee classmate warms hearts across the internet', *Independent*, 1 September. Available at: www.independent.co.uk/life-style/schoolboy-syrian-refugee-friendshipclassmates-video-jack-stanley-rani-asaad-internet-itv-thisa7923991.html

Lauletta, T. (2018) 'Shirtless Tongan Pita Taufatofua finishes ahead of 4 other racers and didn't crash into a tree in his Winter Olympics debut', 16 February. Available at: https://www.businessinsider.com/pita-taufatofua-race-result-winter-olympics-2018-2?r=US&IR=T (accessed February 2020).

Moyer, J. (2017) 'Sometimes people change: Maryland shop covers up racist tattoos for free', *Washington Post*, 22 February. Available at: www.washingtonpost.com/local/sometimes-people-change-marylandshop-covers-racist-tattoos-for-free/2017/02/21/8fec193e-f30a-11e6-8366-98329d93f4ad_story.html?utm_term=.774a1c5132ab

Nordstrom, L. (2017) 'Viking warrior found in Sweden was a woman, researchers confirm', *thelocalsweden*, 8 September. Available at: www.thelocal.se/20170908/confirmed-viking-warrior-was-a-woman

Nsubuga, J. (2017) 'Boy refused princess makeover at Disneyland Paris because he's not a girl', *Metro*, 30 August. Available at: http://metro.co.uk/2017/08/30/boy-refusedprincess-makeover-at-disneyland-paris-because-hes-not-agirl-6890804/

Pengelly, M. (2017) 'White House photo caption omits husband of Luxembourg's gay PM', *The Guardian*, 27 May. Available at: www.theguardian.com/us-news/2017/may/27/white-house-photo-captionsame-sex-spouse-luxembourg-pm

Pittman, T. (2017) 'High school students start club to make sure no one sits alone at lunch', *HuffPost*, 13 March. Available at: www.huffingtonpost.com/entry/high-school-students-start-club-to-makesure-no-one-sits-alone-at-lunch_us_58c6cdb6e4b0ed71826e51b8?utm_hp_ref=power-of-humanity

Pride in London (2017) 'UK Parliament lights up ahead of Pride in London Parade', 7 July. Available at: https://prideinlondon.org/news-and-views/uk-parliament-lights-up-ahead-of-pride-in-london-parade/ (accessed February 2020).

Rawlinson, K. (2017) 'Disneyland apologises for banning boy from princess experience', *The Guardian*, 30 August. Available at: www.theguardian.com/film/2017/aug/30/disney land-apologises-for-banning-boy-from-princess-experience#img-1

Reneau, A. (2019) 'A 6-year-old designed a custom t-shirt for his first day at school and it's seriously the best', *Upworthy*, 8 February. Available at: www.upworthy.com/6-year-old-designed-a-custom-t-shirt-for-his-first-day-ofschool?fbclid=IwAR0gBuoL47JzCI-j_zRKiWR_QegY_U7HYPDAbpvWUqIDn-O3C1pggFcj5DQ

Renstrom, E. (2018) 'Mission unstoppable; inside the all-female trek to the North Pole', *Wired*, 9 June. Available at: www.wired.com/story/inside-all-female-trek-to-north-pole/

Slater, C. (2017) 'Thousands pack Albert Square to remember Manchester terror attack victims', *Manchester Evening News*, 23 May. Available at: www.manchestereveningnews.co.uk/news/greater-manchester-news/thousands-pack-albert-square-remember-13082307

Worley, W. (2017) 'German supermarket empties shelves of foreign-made goods to make a point about racism', *Independent*, 27 August. Available at: www.independent.co.uk/news/world/europe/edeka-german-supermarketempty-shelves-racism-diversity-largest-chain-a7908551.html

Wong, B. (2015) 'Bride's dad stops wedding so stepdad can walk down the aisle too', *Huff-Post*, 30 September. Available at: www.huffingtonpost.co.uk/entry/brides-dad-stops-wedding-so-stepdadcan-walk-down-the-aisle-too_n_560ac699e4b0768126ff4f2b

Chapter 4

NO OUTSIDERS MASTERCLASS

No Outsiders masterclass

This plan was delivered at the Varkey Foundation Global Education and Skills Forum, Dubai, in March 2019 as a masterclass demonstrating a No Outsiders workshop. The lesson can be viewed on YouTube (www.youtube.com/watch?v=skmLOOJqKG4) and could be used as the subject of a staff meeting preceding a discussion about how to use No Outsiders to build community cohesion with children and parents.

The text *Here We Are* by Oliver Jeffers is a wonderful book encouraging the reader to explore and ask questions about the world around us. What is space; what is the sea; what is land; what do we need to live? But for the purpose of teaching about No Outsiders, there is a beautiful focus on people and the differences between them. Near the end of the book the reader realises who the author is speaking to and then the aims of the book are revealed; this is about preparing a child for life in the twenty-first century.

The final pages of the text are magnificent; the child is encouraged to ask questions if they are unsure about anything; 'And if I'm not around,' the author explains, 'You can always ask someone else. You're never alone on earth.'

The masterclass was delivered to an international audience and the aim for me was to demonstrate how a No Outsiders ethos encourages children to ask questions, broaden horizons and reduce prejudice by engaging in dialogue with different people. The plan was adapted from a lesson plan for a parent/child No Outsiders workshop taken from *Reclaiming Radical Ideas in Schools: Preparing Young Children for Life in Modern Britain* (Moffat 2017), but as with every good lesson, the end result weaved away from the intended plan as discussion and debate took the class in different directions. This version of the plan was written in retrospect, after the masterclass.

Text: *Here We Are* – Oliver Jeffers

Learning intention: To consider what we don't know (yet)

Success criteria: I know things/I know I don't know things/I know how I can find out about new things/I am excited about my future

Starter: In 2018 a photo went viral showing racist graffiti transformed into a celebration of different languages. Andersson (2018) reports on the story of
Chris Walker, a resident from Walthamstow who altered an image from MP Stella Creasey's Instagram. The image shows a fence with 'speak English' scrawled across the panels, but Chris has added lots of other languages to the graffiti: Punjabi, French, Romanian, Polish, etc. He has also added the word 'We' in front of the two original words.

Ask the class to discuss with a partner what they see in the image, then feed back.

What is the most important word in the graffiti? (We) Why is 'we' the most important word?

Why do people write racist graffiti? Where do those ideas come from? (fear, they don't understand about diversity and difference; they want everyone to be the same)

What did the person who wrote the original graffiti want people to feel? (frightened, 'you're not welcome here', like an outsider)

There are lots of responses you could make if you saw the original graffiti; you could ignore it or you could paint it out. A MP chose to take a photo and share it on social media – why did the MP do that?

What did Chris do with the graffiti? Why?

How did Chris want people who saw the graffiti to feel? (like they belong) Chris wanted everyone to know they belong and they are welcome.

The original photo with 'speak English' never went viral but the second photo with all the different languages did. What does this show about most people in the UK and their ideas about diversity and difference?

Discussion text: Read *Here We Are*. Ask as you read through the book who is the writer talking to?

At the end ask the class, 'Why did Oliver Jeffers write this book? What message was he trying to convey'?

Show again the last page: 'If you're not sure, ask someone else: you're never alone on earth' what does that mean? What is the author telling us to do? (talk/ask questions)

Why do we ask questions? We ask questions to find out about things because there are some things that we know, some things that we don't know.

Say you have a challenge for the group over the next two minutes; you want everyone in the room to find out something new. How do we do that? We use the resources in the room – each other. Find a partner and find out something new; ask a question. The challenge is to find what you can learn from the person next to you; teach them something but also they need to teach something to you.

Give the group two minutes and then ask people to share what they have learned.

Give each child and their adult time to discuss the book.

Be excited about the fact that we have all just experienced new learning. How did we achieve that new learning? By talking to each other and asking questions.

Main activity: Put the class in to groups of 6–8 and give each group a large piece of paper and paints. Explain the paper represents us here in this room today, but it is blank and needs to be filled. We are going to use art to explore the diversity that exists in this room. Ask each person to think about what they can paint on to the paper to represent them, but they are not going to paint their own symbol; they must paint symbols for other people. How do you find out what to paint? By asking each person how they want to be represented on the paper and then painting it for them. Everyone brings something to the room be it ethnicity, language, religion, culture, talent, ability, experience, likes, dislikes, etc. Each group creates a montage of art to represent the diversity that exists here today. (In the masterclass because of time and space I asked for volunteers at the front to ask different people in the room what to paint and then paint objects for them, rather than ask everyone to paint individually.)

Give the groups time to create their montage. People will have to move around the room to ask everyone what to paint, but how each group organises this is up to them. At the end show the creations: are they the same? Why not? Which pictures best represent our diversity?

Plenary: Why is exploring and accepting diversity important? Why do we need to teach our children in 2020 to love diversity? If people are frightened of difference what can we do? It's our job to explain to people who feel fear that what makes our community great is its diversity. In our community you can have different skin, different faith, different language, a different family, disabilities, different gender, different age and that is what makes our community a fantastic place to live; everyone belongs here and there are no outsiders. We want to live in a world where people are different but they get along, but we have to work at it; how do we achieve it? We achieve it through dialogue and asking questions.

Give the group one final task as they leave the room. Go back to the starter image of the graffiti and say you want us to create our own version. Put up a large piece of paper by the door and paint the name of the city where you are taking the lesson. As people leave ask them to write a word on the paper to show who is welcome in our city.

References

Andersson, J. (2018) 'Racist "speak English" graffiti transformed into celebration of diversity by local artist in Walthamstow', *Inews.co.uk*, 30 November.

Jeffers, O. (2017) *Here We Are*. London: HarperCollins.

Moffat, A. (2017) *Reclaiming Radical Ideas in Schools: Preparing Young Children for Life in Modern Britain*. Abingdon: Routledge.

Chapter 5

OTHER VOICES

Other voices

No Outsiders is working in many schools around the country. The aim of this chapter is to hear from headteachers who have taken No Outsiders and made it a success in their own schools. There is so much brilliant, inspiring work going on in schools and we often don't hear about it. Here are four headteachers who have inspired me with their work.

Helen Mckenna, Newcastle upon Tyne

How did we introduce No Outsiders?

We were invited by the City Council to take part in a one day training session with Andrew and we were given a place for the headteacher, one member of staff and one governor. We loved the simplicity of the programme, the choice of the texts used to deliver it and the values which underpinned every lesson.

Governors agreed that using the programme would add quality to our personal development provision, especially in relation to the Equalities Act.

We told parents and carers via a summer term newsletter that we would be using the No Outsiders scheme in school and informed them that teachers would be able to talk to them in more detail at the class coffee mornings in September. We then invited all parents and carers to a No Outsiders lesson in their child's class where they could observe and participate in the delivery of a session. In most classes, we had excellent attendance and parents gave us very positive feedback; in fact all feedback was positive.

We kept parents and carers informed of our No Outsiders work via the school Twitter and class Twitter accounts and also included pictures and ideas which we had used in assemblies.

What was the impact?

Our pupils very quickly caught on to the language and the concept of No Outsiders and were soon trying to work out how every assembly story was about

No Outsiders, even when they weren't. Pupils brought books to me to ask if I thought they could be used as a No Outsiders book and they loved telling visitors what No Outsiders meant. Staff used the language and concept when dealing with behaviour issues and it became embedded with very little effort. Some parents and carers also started using the language and everyone knew exactly what it was about. We were particularly pleased that we could use language which the children understood to strengthen relationships between different cultural and ethnic groups within school.

Teachers enjoy delivering the sessions because the books which Andrew has identified are all high quality and engaging texts. We have been flexible in our delivery and have added some texts of our own.

Were there any challenges and how did we meet them?

A very small number of families raised questions about the No Outsiders lessons. Through discussion and sharing of the resources, we were able to clarify that the ethos and values around No Outsiders was no different to what school was already doing. However, the benefit of the programme meant that we were able to deliver our teaching about the Equalities Act through high-quality and engaging texts. We emphasised that all lessons, discussions and language used by staff would be age appropriate and sensitive to a wide range of views and backgrounds. We were honest and transparent about the programme and through discussion we were able to clarify some of the misinformation around its aims and content.

Stand-out moments

This spring, we adopted a Little Elmer for the Great North Elmer Parade. This involves the whole school community decorating a large white fibreglass Elmer which then joins a region-wide Elmer parade in the summer. We introduced Elmer to the children in assembly and their response was overwhelmingly in support of decorating the sculpture in a way which would reflect our No Outsiders work and values. Following an assembly about the terrorist attacks in Sri Lanka, a Year 4 child suggested we all put our handprints on Elmer using different colours to show that we are all different and all equal. With the help of one of our governors, we decorated

Elmer with 225 handprints as well as words to reflect the No Outsiders concepts and values.

What next?

In developing our curriculum this coming year, the concepts from No Outsiders will be curriculum drivers as well as the programme being central to the PSHE curriculum. We will also be looking at developing and extending resources so that there is more material available to class teachers.

Of course, we hope that our Little Elmer will spread the message in the wider community and we will be using him to promote the values in and beyond school when he returns to us from the herd!

Troy Jenkinson, Leicester

How did you introduce No Outsiders to your school?

I started working at my current school in January 2016. The school had not worked towards any awards and although it was a friendly enough place, there was an insular culture of low expectations where the common playground insult "that's gay" was rife.

I began by working with contacts in the local authority who helped us to gain the Beyond Bullying accreditation and tackled some of the issues with the help of the school councillors using *And Tango Makes Three* in an assembly. This helped tremendously and as a result, we were asked to join a pilot to bring No Outsiders as a project into schools across Leicestershire and the city.

Simultaneously, I had written some stories to share with children in assemblies to help give children who might be feeling marginalised representation and therefore a voice. One such story, *The Best Mummy Snails in the Whole Wide World* was just being published as a picture book.

Introducing No Outsiders into our school seemed like a no brainer; it is very much a part of my philosophy to talk openly and honestly with children and give them a voice. Picture books are a non-threatening way of doing this.

I attended the training and brought along a governor who was very much on board. I knew she would be an advocate to help convince the rest of the governing body. Once the governors were on board, I led a training session for staff and we wrote to parents as a governing body, inviting them to come in, in small groups, to look at the collection of books to see for themselves what the stories are about. Staff who would be using the books were on hand to answer any questions but nothing unexpected came up.

As the school council had been instrumental in driving the anti-bullying campaign, I wanted them to be part of the introduction of No Outsiders. I arranged to take some of my school councillors to visit Parkfield to 'borrow' some ideas from their No Outsiders approach. We went armed with iPads to get photos of displays etc and to take ideas back to our school. We also joined some of Parkfield's school council to ask them what they thought about the initiative as well as watching an assembly led by Andrew. It is important for me to ensure any changes made to give children a voice are led by the children themselves.

What was the impact?

Firstly, feedback from the visit we undertook at Parkfield was used for the school council to create an action plan of what they wanted to see happening. They wanted assemblies that talked to them about 'grown-up' issues similar to what they had witnessed. The children also drove the monitoring of when classes put up their No Outsiders displays.

Impact has generally been more anecdotal than data focused. When questioned children were able to clearly say why we were a No Outsiders school. One adopted child with same sex parents felt able to ask if she could bring in a book to share as a 'No Outsiders' book and we have branched out into finding other stories we can use now too (including short novels such as Michaela Morgan's *Respect* – the biography of Walter Tull. He overcame a range of prejudices to become the first black professional footballer and high-ranking officer in the First World War. Another child in Year 4 with a tough and challenging home life explained in a picture book he created that it is ok to be transgender. When asked, he was able to explain this as 'when someone is born as a boy but deep down inside, they feel more comfortable being a girl, or the other way around.'

I can give lots of other examples, including when I read *The Best Mummy Snails..*" to the children in assembly after it was first published, I asked the children what they thought the moral of the story was. One Year 6 boy put his hand up and said, "It's easy to say what the moral is, love is love. It doesn't matter whether you love a boy or a girl, as long as you show love. That is important."

Were there any challenges, if so how did you deal with them?

As we were very open with our aims in the first place, there have been very few challenges. One parent apparently stated to a teacher in the Spring parents' evening that she couldn't understand why we had been doing so many 'gay assemblies'. This was referring to one assembly linked to the Winter Olympics where two gay competitors had been snapped by the paparazzi kissing. The news story went viral so it seemed appropriate to discuss it with the children. All the staff had been briefed when we introduced the project to direct any concerns to me as the head to deal with if they felt uncomfortable with tricky questions. The teacher responded (brilliantly) to the parent by saying she felt the No Outsiders books and assemblies had gone down really well with the children and if the parent had any concerns, she was welcome to make an appointment to see me as the head. She never came. The key learning point here is to brief staff with a short, to the point script to use if needed.

How did you develop the ethos?

The No Outsiders ethos has been particularly driven by the pupils and led by the governors. They were instrumental in the initial visits and training. The children have helped to monitor it. They even wanted to create a No Outsiders Policy similar to our child friendly Anti-Bullying Policy the school council created the year before. Giving the children the responsibility to move this forward, they have run with it. Two older children even incorporated it into our review of our Behaviour Policy and Character Education work. The school council ran a competition to design cartoon characters to represent key character trait vocabulary selected to convey our school ethos of Teamwork, Effort, Attitude and Manners. Each of the characters designed by the children and later professionalised by a local children's illustrator, represented people with disability, differing ethnicity and gender. They fostered our key traits of respect and equality for all.

Any 'moments' for you?

We had many moments but one key one was being asked by the local authority to help create a short film to promote the pilot to other Leicestershire schools. One parent who was filmed as part of the pilot stated she had been apprehensive about talking to her son with other children about the fact his father was in a same sex relationship. Being part of the project had given her the strength to stand up and be proud of who her family were, safe in the knowledge her son would be supported.

A second key moment came on the back of the terrible demonstrations that occurred outside the Birmingham primaries. We were approached by the BBC who wanted to film a school who had successfully introduced the project. When I agreed the producer was a little taken aback as most schools were keeping quiet for fear of the protests spreading to their schools. Determined and resolute to stand by colleagues who were facing difficult times, and with the backing of our staff and governors, we set about getting permissions for the children to be filmed. Out of the four classes of children being filmed only a handful of 3 or 4 parents declined permission for their children to be filmed (and this was more about going on the TV rather than opposing the project itself). One such parent took the time to write to me directly after to say how proud she was that her children attended a school that felt able to speak out and stand up for what was right. The subsequent annual parent questionnaire had many responses referring directly to the good work we have been doing as part of the No Outsiders project.

What's next for you and No Outsiders?

As a school we have just helped the local authority launch the next cohort of schools using the No Outsiders materials under the project title 'Everyone's Welcome'. We will be proactively supporting these and other schools. We are now advocates for No Outsiders and would welcome visitors who would like to see for themselves what we do, just as Parkfield did for us. (I openly encourage people to come and visit and you are welcome to include this in your book.) We are continuing to embed the stories into our ethos. We will see what the next academic year brings with the school council's aims but, no doubt, they will want to continue and develop what we have already started. Ideally, we would like to be more vocal in support of those schools who have been and are continuing to go through more challenging times.

The introduction of the DfE's new Relationships and Sex Education policies will hopefully offer a more robust clarity to school leaders about how to prioritise and differentiate between relationships education and sex education.

Personally, I have released a second book, *The Most Contented Snail in the Whole Wide World*, aimed at raising awareness of trans children in our schools. I am visiting schools around the country sharing my books and am looking at ways to get my stories into more schools to help normalise LGBT+ issues.

Cheshire West

In February 2017 I was invited to speak at a Saturday morning event at a school in Oxford by Ed Finch, possibly the most enthusiastic teacher I have ever met! "Oxford Reading Spree" was a fantastic day of discussion for over 100 teachers willing to give up their Saturday to share practice, experience and children's books. More than anything I see this event as kickstarting No Outsiders. Headteacher Simon Kidwell was there, and he went on to take No Outsiders to Cheshire, starting at his own school and then rolling it out across the borough. Two years later over 60 schools in Cheshire are doing No Outsiders and I've been fortunate to be part of two inspirational events that have stemmed from this. In 2019 headteacher Steve Ellis organised a public speaking competition involving 12 local schools with a No Outsiders theme. Steve asked me to sit on the judging panel for the final which was held at a theatre and I was blown away by the bravery in each child but also by the huge educational opportunities inspired by the event.

In the same year headteacher David Wearing organised a No Outsiders art exhibition that ran for a month at Storyhouse in Chester. I visited one Saturday afternoon and was overwhelmed by the work that had gone in to this exhibition;

the art work on display was phenomenal and would inspire any teacher to develop a creative curriculum at a time when art is often squeezed out of the timetable.

I was inspired by both of these events and I am very grateful to have the words of both headteachers included in this book.

Steve Ellis, Cheshire

What were your aims with the competition?

The overall aims were to provide pupils with the practical skills and knowledge necessary to express themselves clearly, with confidence and power, in a variety of speaking situations, speaking about something which caused them perhaps difficulty so that they may feel more confident and stronger about their choices and decisions.

Pupils had the opportunity to be taught presentation techniques; how to plan and structure an effective presentation; how to develop ideas; effective delivery methods; and how to overcome anxiety, fear and nervousness when making a presentation. This was a critical element for me because speaking in public is tricky and it requires practice. Some of the pupils repeated their speech over 100 times in order to perfect it and there is a logic and lesson there for other areas of the curriculum. You cannot be good at something straight away – it requires focus and practice and speaking is one of those skills which requires practice. I myself have listened to great speakers – studied how to speak with positive body language and flow. As an adult I recognise the power of presenting with authority and confidence but pupils in mainstream primary schools are not, in general, offered the opportunity to learn public speaking skills. Coupled with the theme of feeling like an outsider it presents a unique opportunity to open up pupils who have difficulty in talking about either illness, friendship issues, identity and feelings of being an outsider.

How did you organise it?

We used guidance from a range of public speaking examination boards and simply arranged for the children to have an introduction, main arguments and conclusion with an external panel of judges asking questions at the end to clarify any of the points the pupil had made. We gave guidance on the use of non-verbal and verbal skills and also how to use notes or speak with confidence and style. Twelve schools took part over four days with the winners from each day moving forward to a grand final. Three pupils from each school were brought forward from a Year 5 class and there were internal competitions to find the best three from each school.

What was the impact on the children?

Seismic. The impact was seismic and none of the organisers including myself could really appreciate just how many pupils had felt like an outsider. Each pupil spoke with such authority, passion and fire that most adults in the room were shocked. The short term impact on pupils was substantial but I was more interested in the longer term impact. One pupils with junior arthritis has spoken and used the same speech at numerous other adult forums. She has been recognised by doctors and speakers for the manner in which she speaks about an often debilitating disease. Other pupils have found great confidence and solace from speaking about their identity and gained a lot of strength from having acceptance and understanding. Others found speaking about friendship and peer pressure a relief that others knew. It gave pupils a forum to open up to their feelings, their worries and perhaps even their nightmares.

Did you have any comments from parents?

Parents were resoundingly positive. Not one parent offered anything but praise and celebration for the event. Many took to Twitter to praise the schools because they offered their pupils an opportunity which many do not get.

Any 'moments' for you?

I did not realise how important the No Outsiders topic was going to be. The previous year we titled the speeches 'life is a journey and not a destination'. It has nowhere near the impact as the No Outsiders topic. It dawned on me after the first day that children really never talk about these things except in private or to their close friends so to do it in a public forum was frightening but post the fear is a much greater feeling of joy. The impact on self-esteem is so much higher.

Any advice for other teachers thinking about a similar project?

Make sure the pupils chosen are confident enough to speak in public. Some aren't and that is okay. We had some internally in school who didn't and couldn't speak in front of their class let alone in an auditorium. We clapped when they said one word and then cried. But we hugged them and cheered and said well done. Even those children smiled once they had tried.

What's next for you and No Outsiders?

I will continue to organise and lead the No Outsider public speaking competition with the Storyhouse in Chester. It will continue to grow with perhaps more schools involved across Cheshire West and Chester. We have incorporated No Outsiders into all of our Multi-Academy Trust in full (MAT) schools to ensure respect, tolerance and kindness are built into our curriculums so that none of our pupils feels like an outsider.

David Wearing, Cheshire

What were your aims with the No Outsiders exhibition?

There were a number of aims behind the No Outsiders exhibition.

The main aim of the exhibition was to celebrate equality and diversity and to open up discussion and debate both at the exhibition venue – Storyhouse Cultural Centre in Chester – but also online via social media.

It was also to promote the No Outsiders books and to showcase the amazing written and artistic work of pupils and teachers across our three trust schools as well as other schools that joined in.

In addition, I wanted to ensure that the ethos of No Outsiders was shared with a wider audience so that members of the general public had a clear understanding of its aims and objectives. Also, that other teachers and senior leaders would visit to find out more and hopefully emulate in their own settings.

Above all, it was to celebrate that 'No one is the same, but everyone is equal!'

How did you organise it?

I presented my exhibition idea to our three trust schools at a joint INSET training day in September 2018. I outlined the plan and shared some of the books from the No Outsiders books pack with them. Teachers then got into year group teams and planned for a focused No Outsiders writing unit to run in February. Resources were ordered and each school worked for two to three weeks using a variety of books, producing some really thoughtful responses which were displayed in a variety of ways: artwork, made books, small booklets, etc. The work was then collected and curated at the Storyhouse (www.story house.com) for two weeks over the Easter break in 2019, front of house for maximum impact and footfall.

What was the impact?

There were many visitors to the exhibition and a visitors' book collated some lovely comments about both the work and more importantly the No Outsiders ethos. There was a real buzz on social media and Storyhouse really embraced the exhibition and commented on the many visitors it brought to the venue. It has also led many other local headteachers to contact me to find out more so that they can implement No Outsiders in their school. Children were also delighted and proud to share their work with their families when they visited in the Easter holidays.

Any 'moments' for you?

A couple of stand-out moments for me were:

- Proud Marys – a local LGBT+ choir who were performing at the Storyhouse whilst the exhibition was on made the time to visit it and take a photo to share on social media supporting the No Outsiders work.

- Simply seeing individuals picking up books from the collection and finding a quiet space to read and discuss with their child.

Any advice for other teachers thinking about an exhibition?

I would say plan well, make sure you've got a great venue (all schools are great venues too!), give it the time it needs – could be a block of literacy work or a No Outsiders themed month (just to be clear here – we continue to use the books throughout the year and in assembly but made it more of a focus for a fortnight), get a few schools together – connecting is great, share on social media, advertise (we produced a leaflet for parents), ensure that curated work is of a high standard and it showcases the ethos of No Outsiders.

What's next for you and No Outsiders?

I am coordinating a No Outsiders working group with other local heads to keep the momentum going. I am also talking about how my school has approached the Equality Act with other heads, both locally and nationally. It is important that an exhibition isn't a one-off and the end of the journey – I will keep thinking of ideas to support children to know that it is OK to be themselves and to ensure that we all are INSIDERS, not OUTSIDERS.

Chapter 6

A FESTIVAL OF BOOKS

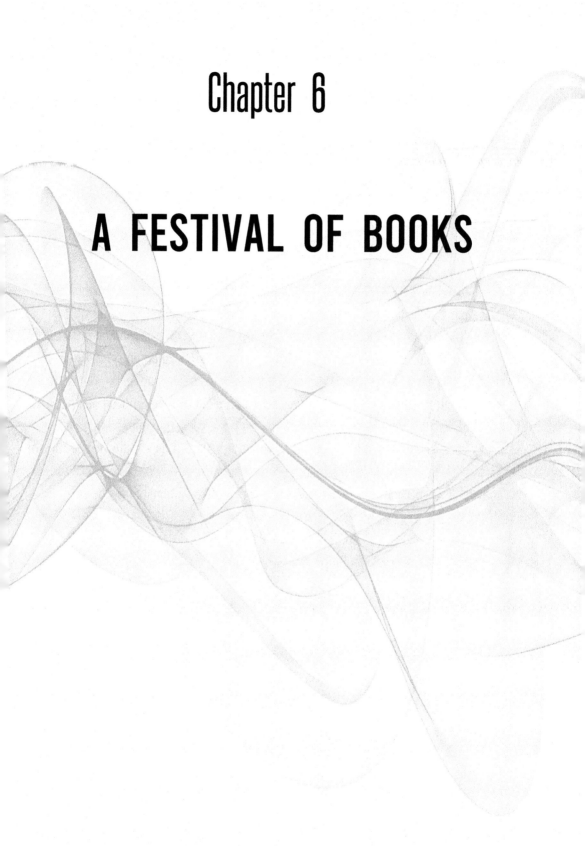

A festival of books

I have thoroughly enjoyed researching which books to include in the 2020 version of No Outsiders. Since writing the last version six years ago there has been a significant rise in the number of great inclusive books to support this work in schools and I've been lucky to have stumbled over Letterbox Library (www.letter boxlibrary.com) who have provided many suggestions over the years for picture books that might develop the ethos.

When planning this No Outsiders scheme the hardest task was deciding what to leave out. Originally there were eight books per year group giving a total of 56 picture books. Those I did have to leave out are available to download on my website (www.no-outsiders.com) – this is to ensure no book feels like an outsider! The website is a place where I often upload recommended books and lesson plans, or replacement lesson plans if books in my scheme go out of print. I have been accused a number of times in recent protests of making huge sums of money through these books because some parents believed I wrote them all… if only! I didn't write any of these books, I simply found them and recommended them. My sincere thanks to the authors of all the books I use for creating such wonderful stimulating stories.

What follows is a brief explanation of why each book was chosen and how it can be used to support a No Outsiders ethos. Of course, each of the books can also be used as a stand-alone story book, and much pleasure can be derived from reading it with a child.

EYFS

The aims in the Early Years Foundation Stage (EYFS) is to introduce the No Outsiders ethos using very simplistic language; we are all different and we are all friends. There is nothing more complicated in the EYFS plans than the message that it's ok to be you and you may be different to me, but that's ok too.

You Choose encourages children to choose their favourite place to live, favourite transport, favourite food, etc and shows that we all like different things. This is explored further in **Red Rockets and Rainbow Jelly** where characters Nick and Sue are shown liking different things throughout the book but conclude by saying they like each other. **Hello Hello** shows different animals with a range of shape and colour who all say 'hello' and no one is left out. **The Family Book** shows children that there are many types of family and then we draw our own family (an exercise I'm sure I would have done in Reception in 1975 – it's nothing new!) and **Mommy, Mama and Me** allows children to understand some families have two mums (or two dads); we talk about the things Mommy and Mama do with their child and ask if our own families do similar things (go to the park, drink juice, kiss goodnight). Finally, **Blue Chameleon** shows a lonely chameleon trying to make friends by changing shape and colour; he thinks you have to look like someone to be friends. At the end Chameleon realises you can be yourself and you don't have to change.

Year 1

In Year 1 we develop the understanding of difference to consider ways in which we might be different and how that can sometimes make you feel. The classic story of **Elmer** shows an elephant who decides to hide his difference but realises at the end he should celebrate it. **Going to the Volcano** takes the children on a joyful expedition to an erupting volcano, and is chosen for its perfect call-and-response narrative and obvious role-play opportunity. The images show a huge range of different characters working together so that no one is left out. **Want To Play Trucks?** focuses on conversations between Jack and Alex, one of whom likes to play with dolls and the other with trucks; 'You can't wear a tutu and drive a crane,' argues Jack, and his reasoning is that 'it wouldn't fit in the driver's seat'. A compromise is made where the doll wears dungarees instead and then Jack and Alex go for an ice cream. This lesson plan teaches children to find solutions to conflict and subtly explores gender expectations at the same time. **Hair, It's a Family Affair** encourages children to celebrate their family and ways their family might be different; the family in the story (who happen to be African Caribbean) have different hair and the character is proud to belong. **My World Your World** explores ways two children are different before finding a way they are similar. I saw a wonderful film clip posted by a school on Twitter showing children doing exactly this in response to this book; 'I like peas, he likes carrots but we both like pizza!' Finally, **Errol's Garden** is a simple celebration of team work; I chose it for no other reason than the main character knocking on his very diverse set of neighbours' doors asking for help and everyone joins in!

Year 2

Can I Join Your Club? explores how Duck feels when animals exclude him from their clubs for not being like them. Duck sets up his own club and everyone is welcome, regardless of the animal noises they make. **How To Be a Lion** shows children that not all lions behave in the same way; Leo is gentle and makes friends with a duck. This book is the first in the scheme to explore peer pressure to behave in a certain way – as the other lions tell Leo be 'more lion', the children are encouraged to empathise with Leo and find a solution. **The Great Big Book of Families** is a celebration of diversity in the UK today; there are families represented but there are also houses, schools, jobs, festivals – it's a great way to introduce the meaning of the word diversity. I was overjoyed to find **Amazing** as it's a snapshot of friendship where the main character uses a wheelchair but the disability is never mentioned, allowing us to demonstrate it's not an issue. **What the Jackdaw Saw** is a subtle way to promote awareness of communication needs as, to ensure all the animals can understand him, the Jackdaw learns to sign with his wings. Finally, **All Are Welcome** feels like it was written for a No Outsiders lesson; I could not have asked for a better representation of the ethos for six-year-olds! The text shows us a diverse class of children who come to school with diverse families, where everyone is welcome.

Year 3

This Is Our House is a perfect story to introduce a No Outsiders ethos to a school; I've used it in many assemblies at the start of term and I'm then able to refer to it throughout the year. In the story, George shuts people out and gives reasons why: because they wear glasses, because they are girls, because they like tunnels. When it is pointed out to George that he has red hair and could also face discrimination, the penny drops – 'This house is for everyone!' he says. This story can be referenced if we talk about terrorist attacks: a child once asked me why the terrorists kill people; 'Because they didn't understand,' I replied. In the story, George doesn't understand, but once it is explained, he changes his mind; anyone can change their mind. **We're All Wonders** is a beautiful story about a boy with facial disfigurement; he is bullied and he dreams of running away. 'What would happen in our school,' the children are asked to consider, 'what would we say if we heard someone being unkind?' We talk about people choosing to be a bystander. **Beegu** gives children an opportunity to explore reasons why the main character, an alien crash-landed on earth, feels like an outsider. Some characters in the story think Beegu does not belong and choose to ostracise the alien; other characters try to make Beegu feel welcome. What would we do if Beegu visited us? Stereotypes are explored in **The Truth About Old People** – what is a stereotype, how do we recognise a stereotype and what can we do if we hear someone being discriminatory? **The Hueys in the New Jumper** is a story I often use when I do a No Outsiders day in schools to introduce the ethos in Key Stage 2. The Hueys are all the same but one day Rupert knits an orange jumper; this causes much consternation and Rupert is treated as an outsider until Gillespie also wears an orange jumper. Gradually the Hueys learn it's ok to be different. The final Year 3 book is **Planet Omar: Accidental Trouble Magnet** which in original publication was called 'The Muslims'. I loved this story and at my school we read it over a half term of Year 3 assemblies. The children loved it and would eagerly wait for the next instalment. There is no lesson plan for this text as it can be read over a period of time but the opportunities for discussion after each chapter about stereotypes, racism, islamophobia, bullying are boundless. Mental health is also referenced as the central character has an imaginary friend.

Year 4

Along Came a Different provides opportunity to discuss attitudes towards race and racism; the red shapes don't like the blue shapes who in turn don't like the yellow shapes or the red shapes. At the key point of the story the shapes draw up a set of segregation rules which give us as a class a basis to work from: what do we think of these rules? How can we rewrite them? **Dogs Don't Do Ballet** teaches children to go for their dreams; everyone tells a dog that he can't be a ballerina, but he proves in the end you can be what you want to be. In **Red: A Crayon's Story**, a crayon who looks red can only colour in blue. This is very distressing for him as he knows he should be red, but he cannot get it 'right'. For us this tale is a fantastic stimulus for discussion about identity and expectations and for teaching children to be who you are. **Aalfred and Aalbert** gently shows how two aardvarks get together, helped by a small blue bird. Some children may realise the aardvarks in the story are two males, but that is not the focus of the lesson plan; rather the focus is recognising loneliness, choosing to help others, finding common ground and understanding how companionship affects mental health. **When Sadness Comes To Call** explores how to recognise feelings of sadness and their impact. The lesson plan focus is on good mental health and how it can be achieved. **Julian Is a Mermaid** tells the story of a small boy wanting to be a mermaid. The key to the story for me is Nan's attitude to her grandson; the reader is led to believe she is going to tell him off for dressing up, but instead she supports and helps him. It is a heart-warming story of difference and acceptance.

Year 5

Kenny Lives With Erica and Martina is a book that that focuses on attitudes towards LGBT+ people and homophobia to tell a story of a family who are literally made into outsiders when a wall is built to block them from the street. The ending is thought provoking and enables a class to ask questions about discrimination and form responses. **Rose Blanche** is a beautifully illustrated story told through the eyes of a young girl in Nazi occupied territory. Rose doesn't understand why the behaviour of people around her changes and when she meets children in a concentration camp, she decides to help them. The story is a perfect vehicle to explore prejudice and the choices people make when faced with danger. **Mixed** leads on from Along Came a Different in Year 4 but this time rather than just writing a set of rules to segregate, the colours construct physical walls and fences to separate people of different race. When two different colours fall in love their example serves as a force to alter perceptions. *How To Heal a Broken Wing* is an Amnesty International book that shows a boy choosing to help a fallen bird; he is the only one to stop and help. We return to the concept first raised in Year 3 of choosing to be (or not to be) a bystander. I wanted to include *The Girls* both as a focus on positive representation of different gender, but also to provide a stimulus for discussing friendship and recognising the importance of companionship. The story therefore provides another mental health reference and there is also a subtle LGBT+ moment. *And Tango Makes Three* is a story about a loving family of penguins adopting a chick, and the family happens to consist of two males. There is a new lesson plan for this text in this scheme, the third different lesson plan available over various schemes of work. For this scheme I have focused on the book being banned in some territories (Hong King; Singapore) and asking why? What is it about this book that move some people to ban it? In doing this we recognise that there are differences of opinion in the world about LGBT+ equality; the activity in the plan encourages children to make up their own mind about the situation.

Year 6

The Year 6 books have a theme of acceptance. *King of the Sky* beautifully explores feelings of being an outsider from the perspective of a young refugee boy. He forms a friendship with an elderly man who teaches the boy to work with homing pigeons; through the pigeons, the boy learns to feel a sense of belonging. *The Only Way Is Badger* is truly a book for our times; a badger builds a wall across the forest and instructs the other animals to be 'more badger'. If they fail, they are thrown over the wall. The ending of the story provides much material for discussions about conciliatory behaviour and consequences of actions. *Leaf* describes fears about the unknown and lack of confidence to find out. A polar bear arrives on an island and rather than talking to him, the other animals hide and talk about him. This theme is revisited in *The Island* which is a powerful study of the power one group of people have over another and the dire consequences of unchecked prejudice. *Introducing Teddy* is a wonderful tale of a teddy bear who comes out as trans halfway through the story. All of Teddy's friends accept her as Tilly, no one questions, and this is the focus of the plan. The final book in the scheme, **A Day in the Life of Marlon Bundo**, provides a fantastic opportunity to talk about democracy, prejudice and LGBT+ equality. A rabbit in the White House wants to marry another male bunny and while all the other animals celebrate the wedding, the leader of the animals says two male bunnies marrying is against the law. The animals have a vote to see if the law should be changed. The focus of the lesson plan is how democracy works.

Book list

You Choose – Nick Sharratt and Pippa Goodheart (London: Picture Corgi, Random House, 2004)
Red Rockets and Rainbow Jelly – Sue Heap and Nick Sharratt (London: Penguin Books, 2003)
Hello Hello – Brendan Wenzel (California: Chronicle Books, 2018)
The Family Book – Todd Parr (New York: Little Brown and Company, 2003)
Mommy, Mama and Me – Leslea Newman and Carol Thompson (Berkley: Tricycle Press, 2009)
Blue Chameleon – Emily Gravett (London: Macmillan Children's Books, 2010)

Elmer – David Mckee (London: Andersen Press, 1989)
Going to the Volcano – Andy Stanton (London: Hodder Children's Books, 2018)
Want to Play Trucks? – Ann Stott and Bob Graham (London: Walker Books, 2018)
Hair, It's a Family Affair – Mylo Freeman (London: Cassava Republic Press, 2018)
My World, Your World – Melanie Walsh (London: Picture Corgi, 2004)
Errol's Garden – Gillian Hibbs (Swindon: Child's Play, 2018)

Can I Join Your Club? – John Kelly and Steph Laberis (London: Little Tiger Press, 2017)
How To Be a Lion – Ed Vere (London: Puffin Books, Random House, 2018)
The Great Big Book of Families – Mary Hoffman and Ros Asquith (London: Frances Lincoln Children's Books, 2010)
Amazing – Steve Antony (London: Hodder Children's Books, 2019)
What the Jackdaw Saw – Julia Donaldson and Nick Sharratt (London: Macmillan Children's Books, 2015)
All Are Welcome – Alexandra Penfold and Suzanne Kaufman (London: Bloomsbury Children's Books, 2018)

This Is Our House – Michael Rosen (London: Walker Books, 1996)
We're All Wonders – R.J. Palacio (London: Puffin Books, Random House, 2017)
Beegu – Alexis Deacon (London: Hutchinson, Random House, 2003)
The Truth About Old People – Elina Ellis (London: Two Hoots, 2019)
The Hueys in the New Jumper – Oliver Jeffers (London: Harper Collins Children's Books, 2012)

Planet Omar: Accidental Trouble Magnet – Zanib Mian (London: Hodder Children's Books, 2019)

Along Came a Different – Tom McLaughlin (London: Bloomsbury, 2018)
Dogs Don't Do Ballet – Anna Kemp & Sarah Oglivie (London: Simon and Schuster, 2010)
Red: A Crayon's Story – Michael Hall (London: Green Willow Books, HarperCollins, 2015)
Aalfred and Aalbert – Morag Hood (London: Two Hoots, 2019)
When Sadness Comes To Call – Eva Eland (London: Andersen Press, 2019)
Julian Is a Mermaid – Jessica Love (London: Walker Books, 2018)

Kenny Lives With Erica and Martina – Olly Pike (London: PopnOlly Ltd, 2019)
Rose Blanche – Ian McEwan and Roberto Innocenti (London: Red Fox, Random House, 2004)
Mixed – Arree Chung (London: Henry Holt, 2018)
How To Heal a Broken Wing – Bob Graham (London: Walker Books, 2008)
The Girls – Lauren Lee and Jenny Lovlie (London: Caterpillar Books, Little Tiger Books, 2018)
And Tango Makes Three – Justin Richardson and Peter Parnell (London: Simon and Schuster, 2007)

King of the Sky – Nicola Davis (London: Walker Books, 2017)
The Only Way Is Badger – Stella J. Jones and Carmen Saldana (London: Little Tiger Press, 2018)
Leaf – Sandra Dieckmann (London: Flying Eye Books, 2018)
The Island – Armin Greder (Australia: Allen & Unwin, 2007)
Introducing Teddy – Jessica Walton and Dougal MacPherson (New York: Bloomsbury Children's Books, 2016)
A Day in the Life of Marlon Bundo – Marlon Bundo and Jill Twiss (California: Chronicle Books, 2018)

Chapter 7

THE RESOURCE

The resource

No Outsiders: everyone different, everyone welcome: EYFS

Table 0.1 To choose what I like

Text: *You Choose* by Nick Sharratt and Pippa Goodheart
Learning intention: I can choose what I like
Success criteria: I can make my mind up and tell you things I like/I can ask others what they think
Starter: Show children the front cover of the book. What does 'you choose' mean? What do you think the book is going to be about?
Main: Read *You Choose*. During the first read through do not ask the children for their opinions.
Role play: Say that you are going to read the book again but this time you want to know what the children think about each page; which objects will they choose? Explain at each page you will stop because you want to ask the children for their opinion.   Ensure all children get an opportunity to say what they would choose. Encourage children to ask each other, 'What would you choose?'
Activity: Under headings 'I like' and 'I don't like' ask children to stick pictures of objects from the story.
Plenary: Say, 'We all had a go choosing today. Was anyone left out? Why do you think it was important that everyone had a turn?' How would you feel if you missed your turn?   Lots of us chose different things; does that matter? Is it OK to like different things? Say that's what you like about this class; we all take turns and even though we like different things we all get on.

No Outsiders: everyone different, everyone welcome: EYFS

Table 0.2 It's ok to like different things

Text: *Red Rockets and Rainbow Jelly* by Sue Heap and Nick Sharratt
Learning intention: It's ok to like different things
Success criteria: I know my friends can like different things to me/I know we can still be friends
Starter: Put up images of different fruit on the board: apples, bananas, oranges, carrot sticks. In pairs children to discuss and choose their favourite. Ask the children in their pairs did anyone have different favourites?
Main: Discuss learning intention. Read the text from start to finish. Ask children in talk partners to recall things Nick liked and things Sue liked. Children feedback. Reinforce: 'What a lot of different things! Were Nick and Sue friends? So even though they liked different things, did they still like each other?'
Role play: Ask children in pairs to think of one thing they both like. For example maybe they both like swings or slides or both like apples or bananas. Each pair feeds back to class. Now double up pairs so children are in fours and do the same. Double the group again and repeat the exercise. Repeat again in larger groups and then as a whole class. As a whole class the teacher should lead the discussion; 'Now look at us; we are all different; there are children here with long hair and children with short hair; children with different colour skin and children with different eye colour and we are all different shapes and sizes. I wonder; even though we are all different, can we find *one thing* we all like?' Encourage children to give suggestions; and encourage others to agree or disagree till you reach a consensus. At the end reinforce how brilliant it is that we are all different yet we all like X. (if children nominate friends; encourage objects instead)
Activity: Draw and label different children in the class; and ask them what they like. Write it under the picture; e.g. Ben likes jelly. Children should also draw themselves and write a sentence about what they like. In the middle of the page write 'We are all friends'
Plenary: Today we found things that we all liked, but there are lots of ways we are different too. In pairs children think of things they like that are different, for example Daniel may like chocolate and Tajein may like peas. Daniel feeds back; 'I like chocolate, Tajein likes peas and we are still friends' Tajein then says, 'I like peas, Daniel likes chocolate and we are still friends'. Can any other children think of ways they are different? Are we still friends?   What would life be like if we all liked the same things? Is it ok to be different?

No Outsiders: everyone different, everyone welcome: EYFS

Table 0.3 To say hello

Text: *Hello Hello* by Brendan Wenzel
Learning intention: To say hello
Success criteria: I know in my class we are not all the same/I know we are different/ I know I can make friends with different people/I know how to make friends.
Starter: Show the front cover of the book – what does it say? When do we use the word 'Hello'? What does it mean? Why do we say 'Hello'? Do you have to know who someone is first to say hello?
Main: Read *Hello Hello* and discuss: • What do you notice about the animals in the book? (all different) • Look at the page 'hello colour, hello bright' – contrast the animals • Why do you think the animals are saying hello to each other? • Many of the animals look happy – why do you think that is? • 'A world to see, a world to know' what does this mean? • 'Where to begin, hello hello' why is 'hello' a good beginning?
Role play: Use photo cards of children or name cards. Say you want to make sure this is the friendliest class in the school where everyone says hello to each other and we are going to practise. Ask a child to select a name card randomly; they approach the child selected and say, 'hello!' before the child replies with a 'hello!' Are the children smiling? Why do you think they smile when they say hello? What signal does a smile give? Ask different children to randomly select a name and approach, smile and say hello. Is this a friendly game to play? How does it make us feel when someone approaches, smiles and says hello?
Activity: Children draw two of the animals in the book or two children in our class with the words 'hello'.
Plenary: What other languages have a word for hello? Do we know any other ways of saying hello? Share with class, search on white board for more examples. Why do all languages have a word for hello? What does that show about different people around the world? Why is hello a great word to use when you don't know someone? (because when you say hello people will usually say hello back) If you are meeting someone new and you say hello, what is a good thing to say next? Extension: the back of the book lists names for the animals used in the book and encourages children to find out more about the endangered species.

No Outsiders: everyone different, everyone welcome: EYFS

Table 0.4 All families are different

Text: *The Family Book* by Todd Parr
Learning intention: All families are different
Success criteria: I know who is in my family/I know all families are different
Starter: Put the word 'Family' on the board – ask children, what is a family?
Main: Read the text from start to finish. Ask children in talk partners to recall the different families mentioned in the book and feed back to class. Ask the children, were there any families in the book that were like your family? Focus on the pages 'All families like to hug each other' – why?
Role play: Show the children a baby doll and explain this baby needs a family – who will look after it? What do babies need? Hugs, care, love. Ask for a volunteer to look after the baby and hand it over to them – praise the child for holding the baby carefully and talking softly to keep the baby calm. Ask the child who they want in their family – child chooses any number of children to be in their family and they pass the baby doll around showing they can care for it. Praise the 'family', and then ask for a new volunteer to look after the baby and choose a new family. Continue till everyone who wants a turn being in a family has had one. Highlight the fact that the families are all different as they are being chosen and reinforce that all families are different and that's okay.
Activity: Children draw their family and label.
Plenary: Today we talked about different families – are all the families in our class the same? What different families do we have? One mum? One dad? Mum and dad? Two mums? Two dads? One nan? Two nans etc? What have we learned today? All families are different and that's okay.

No Outsiders: everyone different, everyone welcome: EYFS

Table 0.5 To celebrate my family

Text: *Mommy, Mama and Me* by Leslea Newman, Carol Thompson
Learning intention: To celebrate my family
Success criteria: I know the people in my family are special/I can tell you who loves me
Starter: Go round the circle, children say their favourite thing to do at home.
Main: Read the text from start to finish. Who is the book about? What do they like doing together? Ask the children, is there anything in the book you like doing together? Which activities are your favourite?
Role play: Make a list with the children of the activities in the book. Can anyone act out any of the activities? Stand in a circle and ask for a volunteer to act out one of the activities; once other children recognise the activity they should join in till everyone is role playing the activity. Exclaim, 'What fun it is when we join in together!'
Activity: Children draw and record a sentence for activities they like doing at home with someone in their family.
Plenary: Look at the child's facial expression on each page – how are they feeling? How do we know? Why do you think the child feels happy? (because Mommy and Mama love the child). Who loves you in your family?

No Outsiders: everyone different, everyone welcome: EYFS

Table 0.6 To make a new friend

Text: *Blue Chameleon* by Emily Gravett
Learning Intention: To make a new friend
Success criteria: I know everyone is different in my class/I can make friends with anyone
Starter: Show image of two friends on board – what is the same about them, what is different?
Main: Read the text from start to finish. Why does Blue Chameleon feel lonely at the beginning? Why does he say hello to all the different objects and animals? How does he feel when everyone ignores him? Why does he give up near the end? What changes to make him happy? How does he feel at the end when the other chameleon says hi?
Role play: Let's all be chameleons – explain we are going to stand in a circle and when you ring a bell/bang a tambourine you want children to come to the middle of the circle, find a new friend and say 'hello' (if there is an odd number ask for one child each game to help you make sure no one is left out by pairing children up). Children go back in to the circle with their new friend. Repeat; each time children must find a different 'friend' and say hello. Can we find 10 new friends?
Activity: Give children blank outlines of two chameleons to colour. The chameleons should be different colours. Give each chameleon a speech bubble so children can write their own greeting.
Plenary: Look at the two chameleons at the end – are they the same colour? No! Are they still friends? Of course! Can you be friends with someone who is different to you? Of course you can!

No Outsiders: everyone different, everyone welcome: Year 1

Table 1.1 I like the way I am

Text: *Elmer* by David Mckee
Learning intention: I like the way I am
Success criteria: I know ways we are different/I know how to make my class welcoming
Starter: Prepare a collage on the interactive white board of children from different ethnic and cultural origins. Include images of children in different clothing. Children to identify differences in appearance between the children shown.
Main: Read the text from start to finish. When Elmer changes, ask the children why is he doing that and what will happen next. Talk about Elmer being different in the story. Did he like being different at the start? How does he try and fit in? Should Elmer try to change the colour of his skin?
Role play: Sit the children in a circle and place a large cut-out of Elmer in the middle of the group. Place a bowl of different colour squares next to the cut-out. Explain we are going to make our very own Elmer to celebrate his difference and show him that if he came to our class, he would be welcome. We are going to celebrate the different colours that make Elmer who he is. He needs to know that it is ok to be different. Ask children to choose a coloured square and glue it onto Elmer. When he is complete hold him up and do a round of applause. Isn't he beautiful!
Activity: Give children three key events from story: the picture where the elephants are asleep and Elmer is thinking, the picture where he covers himself in berries and the picture where the berries are washed off. Children describe how Elmer is feeling at each of the different sections of the story.
Plenary: Why did Elmer want to fit in? If Elmer was in our class what would we do and what would we say to him to make sure he didn't feel like that? Go round the circle asking children to say things to help him to like the way he is. Put Elmer on the wall so if he ever does come to our school he knows he is welcome and that people like him the way he is. What does it feel like to be different? Why do we like different people in our school?

No Outsiders: everyone different, everyone welcome: Year 1

Table 1.2 To join in

Text: *Going to the Volcano* by Andy Stanton
Learning Intention: To Join In
Success criteria: I know we are all different/I know we can play together/I can join in
Starter: What is a volcano? Look at the front cover of the book and discuss what is happening; what do you notice about the characters? Are they the same or different? What are they doing?
Main: Read *Going to the Volcano*. <ul><li>How does the story begin? Who is going to the volcano? How are Jane and Dwayne similar, how are they different? Are they happy to be going together? How do we know?</li><li>Who do they meet first? Why don't they say to the bears, 'You can't come!'?</li><li>On the train there are lots of different animals – who is welcome?</li><li>Who is welcome on the plane?</li><li>A spaceship arrives, is anyone left behind when they all splash through the rain? Why not?</li><li>When all the friends are in hospital, are they helping each other? Why?</li><li>Look at the last page and compare to the first page with just Jane and Dwayne. What do you notice about the characters on the last page? (All different)</li></ul>
Role play: Role play the story; start with just Jane and Dwayne and gradually build up the participants, acting out each action described, till the whole class is standing in a circle waiting for the boom (count down from 10–1 and jump back/fall over when the volcano erupts) then help each other with bandages/plasters in the hospital. As you read each line get the children to call back the repeat during the role play.
Activity: Draw a volcano and a range of characters standing on the top. 'Everyone can come', or 'Everyone can join in', 'Come with us', 'Going to the volcano'.
Plenary: Jane and Dwayne started with just two travellers, how many friends do they end up with at the volcano? Why do you think they have so many friends?   At school do we join in like the characters in this story? Do we leave anyone out? We make sure everyone is welcome and everyone can play.   Why do we say everyone can join in? Why is this story about No Outsiders?

No Outsiders: everyone different, everyone welcome: Year 1

Table 1.3 To find ways to play together

Text: *Want to Play Trucks?* by Ann Stott and Bob Graham
Learning intention: To find ways to play together
Success criteria: I know we might like different things/I can find ways you can join my game/I can make sure no one is left out
Starter: Look at the cover of the book; what do you see? What is happening? What do you think the two children are saying? What might happen next? They are holding very different things; can they play together? How?
Main: Read *Want to Play Trucks?* • The two children like different toys; how are their favourite toys different? • Why does Jack say to Alex, 'want to play trucks?' • When Alex puts his doll in to Jack's truck, why doesn't Jack say no? • Jack and Alex argue about the crane driver wearing a tutu; what is the reason Jack gives? What is Alex's solution? • What do both Jack and Alex agree on?
Role play: Say Jack and Alex remind you of our class because they are different in some ways but they are still friends, and that is just like us! Also we are really good at solving challenges. Put the children into pairs. Now explain you are going to give each pair a different toy and the challenge is to find a game that uses both toys so that no one is left out. Hand out a random object to each child e.g. balls, rulers, playdough, cars, dolls, pencils, lego, building bricks, ribbons, string, lolly sticks, marbles, boxes etc. Encourage the children to create a game out of their objects.
Activity: Children record how they made a new game.
Plenary: What can we learn from Jack and Alex? Why doesn't Jack say to Alex, 'go play somewhere else!' Do you think Jack and Alex would allow other children to join their games? How do you know? Was it hard to think of a new game with your partner? Did anyone find a new game they might play again? What do we say about different children playing different games at our school? Why is this story about No Outsiders?

No Outsiders: everyone different, everyone welcome: Year 1

Table 1.4 Proud to be me

Text: *Hair, It's a Family Affair* by Mylo Freeman
Learning Intention: Proud to be me
Success criteria: I know we are all different/I know I am different/I know how I am different/I like the way I am
Starter: Show the front cover of the book and ask children what they think this story is about. Everyone on the cover has different hair, open the first page where there are many more head/hair pictures. How the hair on this page different? Is there anyone in this class with exactly the same hair as you? Is there anyone with very different hair?
Main: Read *Hair, It's a Family Affair*. • Look at the picture of the class on the first page, what do you notice about the different children and their hair? • Why has Grandma's hair changed? • Look at the picture of Macy's sister and her friends; do you think they are proud of the way they look? How do you know? • How does Mum cut little brother's hair? • Why do you think Mum says hair is a family affair? • What does Macy want to be when she grows up? What does her best friend Troy want to be? • Do you think Macy is proud to have different hair? How do you know?
Role play: In the story Macy tells the class about her family and their different hair. Ask children to think about their family or the people who live in their house; does everyone have the same hair? Do some people wear hats or scarves? In pairs tell each other about the different hair in your family. Ask some children to feed back.
Activity: Children draw a picture of the people in their family with a focus on the different hair. Label each person and think of words to describe their hair.
Plenary: In every picture we see of Macy, she looks happy. Why do you think Macy is so happy? Does Macy feel proud to have different hair? What does Macy know about being different? Why is this story about No Outsiders?

No Outsiders: everyone different, everyone welcome: Year 1

Table 1.5 I share the world with lots of people

Text: *My World Your World* by Melanie Walsh
Learning intention: I share the world with lots of people
Success criteria: I know I live in the world/I know the world is full of different people
Starter: Stand in a circle and play 'The sun shines on'. Say: 'The sun shines on everyone who has black shoes' and everyone wearing black shoes swaps places. Next say, 'The sun shines on everyone who has brown eyes' and everyone with brown eyes swaps places. Repeat for blue eyes, 'who likes bananas', 'who likes ice cream' etc.
Main: Read the text from start to finish. Ask, are there any children in the class who do the same things as the children in the book?
Role play: Play 'The sun shines on' again using the text. Begin with, 'The sun shines on everyone who wears a sari to school' (anyone wearing a sari moves), then 'The sun shines on everyone who wears a warm jacket and snow boots to school', then 'The sun shines on everyone who wears trainers to PE'. Stop and ask, 'How are we different to Kavita? How are we the same as Kavita? How are we different to Jacob? How are we the same as Jacob?' Go through the book playing the game for each pair of children. If no one does the things that the characters share (e.g. riding skateboards) can the class think of anything else they might share with the characters? (e.g. they both like playing outside)
Activity: Give children an image of the world to stick in books. Put up the image of the cover of the book on the white board. Children write a sentence about sharing the world or about different people living together in the world, or copy the cover of the book. Children draw an image of two children with different skin colour/dress next to the world to show an understanding of diversity.
Plenary: What is the world? Hold up a globe. Where do we live? What other countries are there in the world? Has anyone been to another country?

No Outsiders: everyone different, everyone welcome: Year 1

Table 1.6 To work together

Text: *Errol's Garden* by Gillian Hibbs
Learning intention: To work together
Success criteria: I know I can ask for help with my ideas/I know how to ask for help/I can work with different people
Starter: Discuss the front cover; what is a garden? What is a garden for? What can you put in a garden? What different types of gardens do we know about?
Main: Read *Errol's Garden* and discuss: • Look at the different plants on the page where Errol says he's 'so good at it'; does anyone recognise any of the different plants? Are there any of these in your homes? • Look at the people living in Errol's block of flats; what do you notice about the people and families? Are they all the same? How are the families different? • Why do you think Errol asked for help to make his garden? • Why do you think Errol makes a plan? • Why is it good that everyone had different things to bring to the garden? • Why do you think everyone helped?
Role play: In the story we see Errol visit lots of different people and ask for help. We don't hear the words he uses but we do then see the people donating different things to the garden. Ask for a volunteer to be Errol and then put the rest of the children in to pairs; each pair is a family for Errol to visit. Give each family a card with an image of a garden object on it (spade/flower/tree/wheelbarrow/fork/seeds/grass/watering can etc.) Errol will visit each family and ask them to help him build his garden (encourage Errol to be polite and to explain what he wants to do each time); each family can then tell Errol what they will bring to the garden and suggest how they can help. The aim is to develop and foster co-operative dialogue.
Activity: The page in the centre of the book where Errol knocks on doors and asks all the different families for help could be the most important page in the story; why? (Because Errol cannot do this job on his own, he needs help. And no one turns him down; everyone joins in) Look at the people Errol asks; how are they different? Children design their own version of this page showing the different people and families that they could ask to help with their garden. Divide a page in to six boxes to create six different families in their doorways. Or Children work in groups of three or four to design a garden. Think about the different plants you might have in your garden and where they will go. Think about whether a tall tree may block light from smaller plants. Do you need a pond? Which jobs will each of you do in your garden? Children could create a 3D garden as part of D&T.
Plenary: Errol says gardens are always changing; what does he mean? Do you think the people will continue to garden together? How do you know? (the last line is 'So, what will we grow next year?') Why did Errol ask for help? What did the neighbours gain from working together? Why is this story about No Outsiders?

Table 2.1 To welcome different people

Text: *Can I Join Your Club?* by John Kelly and Steph Laberis
Learning intention: To welcome different people
Success criteria: I know we are all different/I can name ways we are different/ I have friends who are different/I don't leave people out
Starter: What is a club, what is a club for? Is anyone in the class a member of a club? Why might someone join a club? Look at the front cover of the book and the body language of the animals – what do you think this story is about?
Main: Read *Can I Join Your Club?* After the story discuss with the children the following questions • Why did Duck want to join a club? • Why did the different animals turn him away? • How did this make Duck feel? • When Tortoise asked to join Duck's club, why didn't Duck check if Tortoise could make a good quack noise? • Tortoise is very different to Duck, why did Duck approve Tortoise? • Why did Duck choose to call the club 'Our Club' instead of 'Duck Club'? • What did the animals learn at the end of the story?
Role play: Ask for a volunteer to set up a club. Start by giving them a sign that says their name e.g. 'Ismail's Club' and ask them to stand at the front of the class and invite people to join. Hopefully children will point out that the club shouldn't be called 'Ismail's Club', it should be called 'Our Club'; if no one does, stop the role play and ask the children whether you have the name correct; what did the animals learn in the story? Cross out the child's name and replace it with 'our'. Now ask children one at a time to approach Ismail and ask to join the club. Ismail should use the line from Duck in the book; 'I have to ask you a question … do you want to be in a club with me? Application APPROVED!' Ismail repeats with lots of different children (Ismail should change 'with me' to 'with us'). Once you have about ten children if you don't want to go through the whole class you could stop the role play and ask Ismail, 'Who is approved for your club?' and get the class to shout 'Everyone!'
Activity: Say to the children what you like about the club we have invented today is that it is full of people who are different; no one is the same but no one is left out! Ask children to create a 'Our club' poster and around the lettering draw children and label differences – identify and celebrate differences in the class first (say the best thing about our class is that we have differences – different skin, eye colour, hair, genders, some wear glasses, some have inhalers etc.). Children shouldn't name individual children from the class with their differences on the poster, rather create a poster showing generic children with differences.
Plenary: When Lion says Duck hasn't got the right roar, why doesn't Duck try harder and learn to roar properly so that Lion lets Duck in the club? Why doesn't Duck learn to make different noises to fit in? What can we learn from Duck? Why is this story about No Outsiders? Who was made to feel like an outsider in the story? What can we do in our school to make sure no one feels like an outsider?

No Outsiders: everyone different, everyone welcome: Year 2

Table 2.2 To have self-confidence

Text: *How To Be a Lion* by Ed Vere
Lesson plan by Andrew Moffat/equalitiesprimary.com
Learning intention: To have self-confidence
Success criteria: I know we are all different/I know sometimes it's hard to be different/I know what self-confidence means/I know how I help someone feel confident
Starter: Show the children the front cover of the book. How do you think lions are expected to behave? If this book was an instruction manual for lions, what would be the first three, most important instructions?
Main: Read *How To Be a Lion* all the way through. At the end discuss: • How is Leonard different?   • Look at the page where Leonard and Marianne walk together; what can we learn from these animals?   • How do you think Leonard feels when the other lions come prowling around?   • Why are the other lions so angry towards Leonard?   • Look at the page where Leonard walks away in the rain – how is he feeling? Why?   • How do you think Leonard feels when he goes back to speak to the other lions?   • 'Why don't you be you … and I will be I.' What does Leonard mean?
Role play: Ask children to think of ways they are different to others in the classroom. Perhaps they like different foods or games; good at football, skipping, swimming, catching, maths, art; perhaps they look different or speak different languages. Once each child has found a 'different' partner stand the children in a circle and ask each pair to meet in the middle one pair at a time. each pair to explain how they are different, then say together, 'You be you and I'll be I – we both belong,' and do a high five.
Activity: Show the page where Leonard has doubts; 'Must I be fierce? Must I change?' Children draw the image and write their response to Leonard to help him feel confident. Encourage children to give examples in our school of ways we are different or unique, but we work together. Children could explain what No Outsiders means and how it relates to this story.
Plenary: Why does the author end the book with a question? What is the author trying to encourage the audience to do? How would you answer the question?   Why is this story about No Outsiders? If you see someone feeling unconfident or feeling like an outsider, how can you help?

No Outsiders: everyone different, everyone welcome: Year 2

Table 2.3 To understand what diversity is

Text: *The Great Big Book of Families* by Mary Hoffman and Ros Asquith
Learning intention: To understand what diversity is
Success criteria: I understand what diversity means/I know how my school is diverse
Starter: What is diversity? If children don't know, tell them it means everyone being different. Children to come up with different people who are welcome in our school, and feed back
Main: Read the text from start to finish. At the end ask the children how the book helps us to understand what diversity is. What examples of diversity are there in the book?
Role play: Show the children cards with the following headings: **transport, celebrations, jobs, families, homes, religions**. Explain we are going to play the diversity game. One child takes a card and reads it out, then the child next to them thinks of an example, the next child thinks of another example etc till we run out of ideas. Put the score on the board (so if the child reads celebrations children might say Eid, Christmas, Diwali, giving three points), Can we beat our diversity score on the next card? (For the families card ask children to think of different families in the book – mum and dad, dad and dad, mum and mum, one mum, one dad etc)
Activity: Tell the children it's great to live in the UK because we are so diverse. Give the children an outline of the UK map and around it children record ways in which we celebrate diversity – different religions, different families, different genders etc
Plenary: Imagine if we lived in a place where everyone was the same and did the same things every day – what would it be like? Are lots of countries diverse? Why is diversity a good thing?

No Outsiders: everyone different, everyone welcome: Year 2

Table 2.4 To think about what makes a good friend

Text: *Amazing* by Steve Antony
Learning Intention: To think about what makes a good friend
Success criteria: I know what a friend is/I know how to be a good friend
Starter: Write 'Friend' on the board, ask children in pairs to come up with a definition of a friend. How do you make a friend? How do you stay friends with someone?
Main: Read *Amazing*. Discuss: • Zibbo has lots of friends; how do we know this? • What does Zibbo do with his friends? • Look at the page 'we laugh, we sing etc,', could you join in with Zibbo? Do you do all those things too? • Look at the page where Zibbo goes to the party. What do you notice about the children; are they all the same? How are they different? Are they having fun together? Would you like to go to this party? • 'Zibbo may be different, but he's still my best friend' – how is Zibbo different? • How is Zibbo the same as his friends?
Role play: Some people might say that because Zibbo is different, he should not play with the children in this story. Some people might say Zibbo doesn't belong. In the story he pops the ball and he can't blow out candles safely! How do you think the children in the story would respond if they heard that? Say to the children you are going to argue with them that Zibbo does not belong in your class. Put the children into pairs and give them five minutes to prepare answers. The children may agree with you, or the children may disagree; their job is to use their pupil voice and either stand up for Zibbo or agree that Zibbo should go. Give preparation time and make the following statements and encourage children to answer you. • Zibbo popped the basketball. He cannot play with you. • Zibbo is not safe around candles. The girl holding the cake might have been hurt. • Zibbo is not like you, he is different from you and does not belong here • Zibbo would be happier in a place where there are other dragons like him. (The aim is that children will stand up for Zibbo and argue for him to stay. However children may agree that Zibbo should go. If the class starts to argue that he should go, show them the process of you changing your mind slowly, as you 'realise' that our class is

Table 2.4 (continued)

full of difference and Zibbo is just another example of difference. What does no outsiders mean? It means we are all welcome and Zibbo needs to feel welcome too.)
Activity: Use the page 'We laugh, we sing, we learn' as stimulus for a response about what we do in our class together. Divide the page in to four sections and in each one draw/write about an activity that we all join in. The title is: We do everything together, my class and me.
Plenary: Why do you think the story is called 'Amazing'? Look at the last line – why does Zibbo say, 'And so are you'? Who is amazing in this class? Reinforce you think all the children are amazing; tell them things you are proud of and why you like being their teacher. If Zibbo was in our class, what would we say? Would he feel welcome? Why is this story about No Outsiders?

No Outsiders: everyone different, everyone welcome: Year 2

Table 2.5 To communicate in different ways

Text: *What the Jackdaw Saw* by Julia Donaldson and Nick Sharratt
Learning intention: To communicate in different ways
Success criteria: I know there are different ways to communicate/I can learn to use sign language
Starter: What is sign language? When is sign language used? Who can use sign language?
Main: Read *What the Jackdaw Saw*, discuss why all the animals in the story touch their head when Jackdaw speaks to them. What does touching your head mean in sign language? Why do you think the animals use sign language to communicate with Owl? Why does Jackdaw use sign language at the end of the story?
Role play: Put the children in to a circle and ask for a volunteer to be Jackdaw. Jackdaw flies around the circle asking children to come to the party. Each child tries to warn Jackdaw about the storm using signing. Look at the sign words at the back of the book; children could choose 'storm' or 'danger' signing. After a few children have tried to warn Jackdaw, have everyone blow and make lightning and thunder actions to make a storm. Jackdaw falls to ground. Then ask for someone to pick up Jackdaw and explain what everyone was trying to communicate. Everyone teach Jackdaw how to sign storm/danger. Show Jackdaw how to sign 'Thank you' (fingers to chin and bring fingers forward like blowing a kiss but below the mouth).
Activity: Does anyone in the class know signing? Can they teach the class some words? Look at the sign words listed at the back of the book. Practise as a class. Children record by drawing and labelling diagrams the signs for danger and thank you.
Plenary: Why is learning to sign useful? Why should people who are not deaf learn words in sign language? If someone came to our class who was deaf, how might they feel? What could other children do to make sure no one felt like an outsider?

No Outsiders: everyone different, everyone welcome: Year 2

Table 2.6 To know I belong

Text: *All Are Welcome* by Alexandra Penfold and Suzanne Kaufman
Learning intention: To know I belong
Success criteria: I know who I am/I know there are special things about me/ I know I am different/I know I belong
Starter: Show the children the front cover of the book. Describe the two characters on the cover; how are they similar, how are they different. Look at the title of the story, what do you think the story is going to be about? Look at the inside cover; what clues are there about the story?
Main: Read *All Are Welcome* and discuss: <ul><li>Look at the first page, there is a classroom with 'welcome' on the board. What do you notice about the people in the picture (all different) how are they different?</li><li>Use the different pages as stimulus for discussion; how do we start our days?</li><li>Have some of us come from far away? Do we eat different foods?</li><li>Look at the page 'We're part of a community. Our strength is our diversity' – what does this mean?</li><li>Look at the last page with all the families, what do you notice about the different families?</li><li>What do the words on the last page mean? Why did the author choose to finish the book in this way?</li></ul>
Role play: Look at the page where the children sit at their desks. How do you think the children are feeling? How do you know? Sit the children in a circle and find ways to show how we work together. Try a Mexican wave, pass high fives around the circle; how fast can we pass a clap around the circle?
Activity: Make a class version of the front cover. Ask each child to draw a self-portrait and cut it out to stick on a display saying 'We are all welcome' or each child to draw their own version showing how different children are welcome in their class.
Plenary: Why is this book about No Outsiders? How do we make sure in our class we are all welcome? What sort of things can we do or say every day to make sure no one feels left out? It's great that everyone is this class knows they are welcome but how do we make sure everyone in our school knows they are welcome?

No Outsiders: everyone different, everyone welcome: Year 3

Table 3.1 To understand what discrimination means

Text: *This Is Our House* by Michael Rosen
Learning Intention: To understand what discrimination means
Success criteria: I know how someone can feel like an outsider/I know how to make sure there are no outsiders in my school
Starter: Show image of children on playground. Identify children in the picture who are included and children in the picture who are excluded – how can you tell?
Main: Read the text from start to finish. What are the reasons George gives for not allowing people into his house? What does discrimination mean? How is George showing discrimination? What does the term 'outsider' mean? Who is made to feel like an outsider in the story? How does George change at the end of the story?
Role play: Ask children to write on a label one thing about them; what they like doing or their faith or their ethnicity etc. When all children are wearing labels, tell them you are going to play the part of George in the story. Explain this is going to be very hard because George says things that you would never say. Wear a hat when you are speaking as George so that when you take off the hat you are back as yourself and the discriminatory things George says are gone with the hat. Show the children a mat at the front of the class and explain this is your house. Now ask children one at a time to come to your house and ask to come in. Tell each child they cannot come in because of their label – 'There are no Christians in my house', or, 'There are no black people in my house' or 'People who like football are not welcome in my house' etc. There will be a reaction from the children but remind them that this is what George says. After four or five, take off the hat and tell the children how hard that was for you because those lines were things you have never said and that have no place in our school. Throw the hat away and show the children that you never want to have to wear it again. Now ask the same children you had before to come back and ask again; this time say, 'Of course! Christian people are welcome in my house', or, ''Of course, black people are welcome in my house' etc. At the end, exclaim how much better you feel now that everyone is welcome and no one faces discrimination.
Activity: Children design a poster with the title 'This is our school!' Children demonstrate on the poster that everyone is welcome in our school and there are no outsiders.
Plenary: What can we learn from this book? How can we make sure no one feels like an outsider in our school?

No Outsiders: everyone different, everyone welcome: Year 3

Table 3.2 To understand what a bystander is

Text: *We're All Wonders* by R.J. Palacio
Learning intention: To understand what a bystander is
Success criteria: I know everyone has differences/I know what unique means/I know how people can feel hurt/I know what a bystander is/I know what to do if I see someone being unkind
Starter: What does unique mean? How can a person be unique? What does bystander mean? (when someone sees something they know is wrong but chooses not to say anything or do anything) In what situation might someone be a bystander? Tell the children, there is one part of the story where we see children act as bystanders; at the end of the lesson you will ask for children to identify that part.
Main: Read *We're All Wonders*. Auggie says he is not an ordinary kid; in what ways is Auggie ordinary and how is Auggie different from other kids? Why are Auggie's feelings hurt? Why does Auggie say he is a wonder? Why does Auggie say he wants people to change the way they see? Look at the page where the boy holds out a ball to Auggie; what's changed for Auggie on this page? Which part of the book shows people being bystanders? What needs to happen here?
Role play: We are going to practise using our pupil voice and choosing not to be bystanders. In this story Auggie is called names for being different and everyone acts like a bystander because no one uses their pupil voice to speak up for him. Ask for a volunteer to be Auggie and give out cards to every other child. All the cards are blank except for a small number which have a star on them. Explain to the children that we are going to role play the part of the book where children choose to be bystanders but some of us are going to practise choosing not to be bystanders. If your card is blank, for this role play you need to remain a bystander but if you have a star you need to choose to use your pupil voice and speak up for Auggie. Tell the class you cannot ask anyone to pretend to be unkind towards Auggie so you will take that role. You are going to tell Auggie he is different and doesn't belong here but then say you want to hear people who have stars speak up, use their pupil voice and defend Auggie *(you might want to rehearse some ideas first)*. Repeat the role play with different children being Auggie and different children speaking up. For the last one don't give out cards and say you want everyone to speak up. Praise the class for not being bystanders and using their pupil voice.
Activity: Children draw 'Don't be a bystander' posters showing different responses to bullying.
Plenary: In the story when children call Auggie names why doesn't Auggie use his pupil voice and speak up? Ask children who role played being Auggie how they felt when you said they were different and didn't belong, and how they felt when children used their pupil voice. Discuss what children can do if they see bullying (tell an adult, remove the child: ensure children have strategies).

98

No Outsiders: everyone different, everyone welcome: Year 3

Table 3.3 To be welcoming

Text: *Beegu* by Alexis Deacon
Learning intention: To be welcoming
Success criteria: I know the behaviour that makes someone feel like an outsider/I know how to me someone feel welcome
Starter: Write up the word 'Outsider' and ask children in pairs to make a list of behaviour or situations that make someone feel like an outsider. Children feed back; write up on board to refer to later in the lesson.
Main: Read the text and discuss what happens in the story. How does Beegu feel in the story? (like an outsider) Why? (people make him feel unwelcome) How do people make Beegu feel unwelcome?   Who does make Beegu welcome in the story? (the children) Why do you think the children make Beegu feel welcome? At the end Beegu says he will remember the little ones – what does he mean and why does he say that?
Role play: We are going to play the welcoming game. Send a child out as the detective and while they are gone identify one child to be the welcoming child. Arrange the children in a circle and ask the detective to come back in. The job for the detective is to find the welcoming child within five guesses. The detective approaches a child and says, 'Hello'; if the child is the welcoming child, they reply, 'Hello! Come and stand with me', and move aside to let them in the circle. However, every other child turns away when approached and ignores the detective. Can the detective find the welcoming child?
Activity: Look at the list made at the start of the lesson, of situations where people are made to feel like an outsider. Children record a situation and their response to demonstrate that they know how to stop someone feeling like an outsider, and know how to make someone feel welcome.
Plenary: Ask children to feed back some of their responses. How do we make sure in our school that there are no outsiders? How do we make sure where we live that there are no outsiders? Every morning when we come to school and meet different people on the playground, do we say, 'Good morning!' to everyone? Shall we do that tomorrow?

No Outsiders: everyone different, everyone welcome: Year 3

Table 3.4 To recognise a stereotype

Text: *The Truth About Old People* by Elina Ellis
Learning intention: To recognise a stereotype
Success criteria: I know what a stereotype is/I know how stereotypes affect people/I know everyone is different
Starter: Show an image on the board of a child with an elderly person. Discuss differences and similarities between the two people. Ask the children what they know about old age; what can an elderly person do that is different to us? Is there anything an elderly person cannot do? Show the cover of the book; what do you think this book is about?
Main: Read *The Truth About Old People* and discuss • What is a stereotype and how are stereotypes used in this book? • Why do some people say old people are not much fun? • What does the boy in the story think? • Why do some people say old people are slow? • What does the boy in the story think? • Why do some people say old people are clumsy? • What does the boy think? • Why does the boy think his grandparents are amazing? Consider why the author has chosen to use illustrations as a response to each stereotype rather than having the boy say, 'But I disagree'. What do the illustrations allow the reader to see?
Role play: In the book are a list of stereotypes about old people. Some people think that people are all the same; some people think that old people are all the same, or that boys are all the same or that girls are all the same, or that people who have different skin or religion are all the same. What is the best thing to do if you hear someone using a stereotype? (tell them it's not true) Explain there are many stereotypes about boys and girls. Prepare a selection of cards; on each card write a stereotype e.g. Girls like pink, boys like blue/girls like dolls, boys like cars/girls like skipping, boys like football/ boys like mess, girls like keeping tidy/boys are good at maths, girls are good at drawing/girls can cook, boys can't cook/men go to work, women stay at home and look after children. Lay the cards out face down on the floor and ask children one at a time to pick one and read it. How does it feel to hear the stereotype? What can we say if we hear someone say that? Practise responses to stereotypes.
Activity: Use the book as stimulus, ask children to think of a stereotype and write it down, but instead of writing a response, draw a response in the way the book does. For example, 'Girls don't play football' and a picture of a girl scoring a goal.
Plenary: Why are the illustrations more effective than arguing back in response to a stereotype? If we don't respond to stereotypes, what can happen? Why is it important to respond when we hear someone using a stereotype? Today we have talked about gender stereotypes, but what other stereotypes might we hear?

No Outsiders: everyone different, everyone welcome: Year 3

Table 3.5 To recognise and help an outsider

Text: *The Hueys in the New Jumper* by Oliver Jeffers
Learning intention. To recognise and help an outsider
Success criteria: I know why it's hard to be different/I know how to help someone to be strong
Starter: Show the children the image at the start of the story where all the Hueys are the same. What would it feel like if you lived there but thought things should be different? What would stop you from speaking out?
Main: Read the text from start to finish. Children discuss in talk partners how to come up with a description of what the story is about. Each pair to feed back, 'The new jumper is about …' Discuss what happens to Rupert throughout the story; does he feel happy throughout the whole story? Why not? What does the expression 'stood out like a sore thumb' mean?
Role play: Role play the section of the story where Rupert first wears a new jumper. Have group of three, one child Rupert, one child telling him to take it off and one child Gillespie supporting Rupert. Give Rupert a new jumper to wear. Is it easy to show empathy? How would Rupert have felt if Gillespie hadn't been around? What was the impact of Gillespie showing empathy on Rupert and on the rest of the Hueys? Alternatively you wear a new jumper and ask children first to role play the Hueys being shocked (ask children to recognise how this behaviour makes you feel) then ask children to role play what Gillespie does and discuss the different ways that makes you feel.
Activity: Ask children to focus on four different events in the story: one where Rupert is first wearing his jumper; one where the Hueys are pointing at him in horror; one where Gillespie knits a matching jumper; one where lots of Hueys are wearing jumpers. Children use images either as stimulus for a recount or to write sentences under each describing how Rupert is feeling and explaining why.
Plenary: Why do you think Oliver Jeffers wrote this book? What does he want us to do in our lives? Why do you think the Hueys react so fiercely towards Rupert when he first wears his new jumper? Do you think they are scared? What message would you give to the Hueys?

No Outsiders: everyone different, everyone welcome: Year 3

Table 3.6 To consider living in Britain today

Text: *Planet Omar: Accidental Trouble Magnet* by Zanib Mian
Learning intention: To consider living in Britain today
Success criteria: I know what Britain is/I know where I live/I know lots of different people live in Britain today/I know why some people are scared of difference
Lesson plan: We read this story over a couple of weeks to Year 3 classes and they loved it. Rather than provide a lesson plan for each chapter or event, I enjoyed talking with children after each chapter about character and story development.   The story is rich with discussion points and possible predictions/outcomes.   Some characters change their minds about people and prejudice during the story; use these sections to explore why.
Plenary: Use the story to talk about the different families that live in the UK today and why this makes Britain a great place to live; everyone different, everyone welcome.

No Outsiders: everyone different, everyone welcome: Year 4

Table 4.1 To help someone accept difference

Text: *Along Came a Different* by Tom McLaughlin
Learning intention: To help someone accept difference
Success criteria: I know we are different/I can tell you ways we are different/I know why some people are afraid of difference/I can help people to accept difference.
Starter: Look at the cover of the book; what do you see? Look at the language used and the images; what do you think this story is about? The title doesn't make sense; what is missing from the title sentence? Why do you think the author has chosen this title?
Main: Read *Along Came a Different*. Discuss and feed back: • Why do all the colours think their colour is the best? • Why do they start to separate and make rules? • Why doesn't anyone say they don't agree?
Role play: Give out cards to children, children have either red, yellow or blue cards. Ask children to move in to groups according to colour so that every group has their own space. Now put the following rules up on the board: • Each colour to stay in their own area • Blues can only talk to Blues, Reds can only talk to Reds, Yellows can only talk to Yellows. • No talking to each other • No sharing • No being friends Ask the groups to discuss what they think of the rules and to feed back to the class. Say to the class you are the teacher so it's your job to enforce the rules but of anyone disagrees then now is the time to say. Say to the children if children want to change the rules they need to explain why. Discuss the rules as a class and write new rules if children decide that is what is needed. Note: if children decide they want to keep the original rules, skip to the plenary and discuss what happened in the book when different colours and shapes joined the story. What did the colours learn? Look at the faces when the rules are up and contrast to faces at the end of the book – why are they all happy at the end of the book
Activity: Children work in pairs to cut out different colour shapes, stick them on to a poster with a title, 'Being different is the best thing ever!'
Plenary: Discuss what happened in the book when different colours and shapes joined the story. How did life change for the colours? What did the colours learn? Look at the faces when the rules are up and contrast to faces at the end of the book – why are they all happy at the end of the book At the start of the story, why did the colours think they couldn't be friends? Why do the colours say at the end, 'Being different is the best thing ever!'? How are we different in our class? What can we learn from this book? Why is this book about No Outsiders?

No Outsiders: everyone different, everyone welcome: Year 4

Table 4.2 To choose when to be assertive

Text: *Dogs Don't Do Ballet* by Anna Kemp and Sarah Oglivie
Learning intention: To choose when to be assertive
Success criteria: I know what assertive means/I know why being assertive is sometimes hard
Starter: Write up 'Pupil Voice' on the board: what does it mean? Do we have pupil voice at school? Give examples. Why is it important to speak up and be heard?
Main: Read *Dogs Don't Do Ballet*. What is the message in the story? How does the dog feel when people say he can't do ballet? Why do you think people say that? Look at the image on the page near the start where the girl sits on the step: 'My dog thinks he's a ballerina.' How do you think the girl is feeling? Do you think she loves her dog? Does she try to stop him? What helps to make people change their minds at the end of the story?
Role play: Imagine something you really like doing. How would you feel if people told you couldn't do it but gave no explanation? Ask for a volunteer to reveal something they love to do e.g. play football. Now the child approaches children in the circle and asks them to play football; each child replies 'Don't be silly; children don't play football', or 'You can't play football, it's not allowed!' At this point the volunteer should not answer back, rather they should move on to another person. Repeat four or five times and then ask the volunteer what it feels like to have so many people say football is not allowed. Does it make you want to play regardless or change your behaviour? Repeat with different children and different likes. For the last role play ask someone to be assertive and reply to the people saying the activity is not allowed. Is it hard to answer back when everyone disagrees? Can you answer back and keep calm without getting angry or shouting?
Activity: Write a letter to the dog giving him advice. If you think he should give up the ballet tell him so and explain your reasons. If you think he should continue tell him why and give an explanation (This could be used as an example of persuasive letter writing).
Plenary: What does being assertive mean? Is it difficult to stand up for yourself if everyone around is telling you that you are wrong? Is it easier to just do things people tell you so you fit in? Why do some people just fit in without speaking out even if they don't like something? What is the right thing to do? How can we make sure in our school people are allowed to be who they are without worrying about being different?

No Outsiders: everyone different, everyone welcome: Year 4

Table 4.3 To be proud of who I am

Text: *Red: A Crayon's Story* by Michael Hall
Learning intention: To be proud of who I am
Success criteria: I know why people sometimes don't speak up/I know everyone in my school should be proud of who they are
Starter: With a partner make a list of as many colours as you can – who in the class has the most?
Main: Read and discuss *Red: A Crayon's Story*. What did the red crayon find difficult? What made everyone think he was red? What colour was he inside? How did other characters try to help him become red? Make a list of advice from different characters – Mum/teacher/grandparents – why did his grandparents give him a red scarf and not a blue scarf?
Role play: Give nine children flash cards with lines from the book where 'everyone seemed to have something to say' (see above). Identify a child to be Red and give them a red cape to wrap around them. Now explain Red keeps doing blue things; let's hear what everyone around him is saying. Ask Red to stand in the middle of the circle and have each child with a flash card approach and read out their line. At the end ask children how Red is feeling (confident/unconfident?) and whether the lines in the book were helpful to him?   Now ask everyone to think of a different line to say to Red to make him feel confident again. Ask children to approach Red and say their new lines to make him feel confident again.
Activity: Draw Red in his red cover and write your new advice for him. Should he continue trying to be red? Why/why not?
Plenary: Who in the story changes everything for Red? (The Berry crayon asking him to make a blue ocean). How do you think that changed Red's life? Look at what his mum says on the last page (Olive says, 'My son is brilliant!') how do you think that makes Red feel? At the end he seems to change his name – why? Does Blue now feel accepted and proud? Why? How can we make sure at our school that everyone feels proud to be who they are?

No Outsiders: everyone different, everyone welcome: Year 4

Table 4.4 To find common ground

Text: *Aalfred and Aalbert* by Morag Hood
Learning intention: To find common ground
Success criteria: I know there are more things that we have in common than divide us
Starter: The MP Jo Cox once said, 'We are far more united and have far more in common with each other than things that divide us.' What does this mean? Can anyone think of an example?
Main: Read *Aalfred and Aalbert* and discuss: Why don't Aalfred and Aalbert meeting up at the start of the story? How do you think they feel being alone all the time? 'I might quite like to be part of a pair' why does Aalfred say that? Why does the little bird decide they must meet? What is the plan?   Why does Aalfred want to cheer the bird up? How do Aalfred and Aalbert feel at the end of the story compared to the start? Are they happier at the end or the start? How do we know?
Role play: The bird recognises Aalfred and Aalbert are lonely and tries to think of things they have in common so they can make friends. Does the bird ever talk to either Aalfred or Aalbert? Do you think talking might have helped?   Do you know what things we have in common in our class. Look around, are there people in the room who have things in common with you? Who likes pizza? There you go, things in common all ready.   Give each child a copy of worksheet 4.4A. The target for each child is to find two names in the room to write in each box, thereby finding common ground between two different people.
Activity: Under the heading 'More things in common than things that divide us' make a poster to demonstrate community cohesion. In what ways are we different? In what ways can we work or play together?
Plenary: Aalfred and Aalbert might have stayed on their own for the rest of the story; do you think they would have been happy? How do friendships affect the way we feel about ourselves? How would you feel if you spent the whole day at school and no one spoke to you? What does isolated mean? How can we make sure no one feels isolated at school?

No Outsiders: everyone different, everyone welcome: Year 4

Table 4.4A More things in common

Has a brother	Knows what 9x8 is	Can play an instrument	Favourite colour is red
Has been on a plane	Likes bananas more than apples	Walks to school every day	Can whistle
Member of a club	Can count to ten in another language	Has a sister	Has been to a different country
Likes strawberry ice cream	Has moved house	Has a pet	Can swim

No Outsiders: everyone different, everyone welcome: Year 4

Table 4.5 To look after my mental health

Text: *When Sadness Comes To Call* by Eva Eland
Learning intention: To look after my mental health
Success criteria: I know what mental health is/I know what situations can affect my mental health/I have strategies to look after my mental health
Starter: What is mental health? (ask what dental health is as a way in if children are unsure) Look at the inside cover of the book; what do you see? How are people feeling? (explore wider vocabulary than just 'sad')
Main: Read *When Sadness Comes To Call* and discuss: • Why has the author chosen to represent sadness in this way? • Why does sadness arrive 'unexpectedly'? • 'You try to hide it but it feels like you've become sadness yourself' – what does this mean? • What advice does the author give on how to deal with sadness? (Give at a name, listen to it, ask where it comes from and what it needs) Why does the author say this? • The author suggests taking sadness for a walk, listening to music, drinking hot chocolate – why? • 'Today is a new day' – why has the author chosen to end with this line?
Role play: The author suggests recognising sadness and talking: 'Maybe all it wants to know is that it is welcome'. We are going to practise speaking up, using our pupil voice and sharing our feelings when we need to. In the book the character tries to hide sadness away but it doesn't work – why not? Ask the children to think, when was the last time someone said to them, 'Are you ok?' When was the last time they asked someone else, 'Are you ok?' If someone says, 'I feel sad' or 'I feel lonely,' what is a good response? Discuss (a good response is 'Can I help?' or 'Do you want to talk about it?') Put the children in to pairs and ask them to label themselves A and B. A is the character in the book; think about a reason for their sadness. B is a friend who wants to help. Ask B to offer help by starting a conversation with 'Are you ok?' and then encourage the children to talk. Encourage B children to offer help by developing the conversation. The aim is to encourage children to think about how to have conversations rather than to have to find solutions.
Activity: Say we want to develop a culture in our class where talking about and recognising our feelings is ok. Children to design a poster to encourage others to speak up. A good title would be 'Are you ok?' but children may think of others.
Plenary: Sometimes people pretend to be happy when inside they feel sad; why do they do that? Look at the inside cover at the back of the book and compare it to the front; what has changed? How have the characters dealt with their feelings of sadness? What is mental health? Why is good mental health important to us? Why is this about No Outsiders? (Feeling like an outsider is not good for our mental health; we need to make sure no one feels like an outsider in our class)

No Outsiders: everyone different, everyone welcome: Year 4

Table 4.6 To show acceptance

Text: *Julian Is a Mermaid* by Jessica Love
Learning intention: To show acceptance
Success criteria: I know there are different ways to dress/I know people can choose what they wear/I know different people in my community wear different things/I am accepting of difference
Starter: Show on the board pictures of different people wearing different clothes. Include traditional dress, religious dress, school uniform, fancy dress, formal wear etc. Ask children to consider what the different clothes are for, when each might be worn and for what purpose. When people wear these clothes, do they change? Do the clothes change a person? Do clothes define a person? Can you tell what a person is like from the clothes they wear?
Main: Read *Julian Is a Mermaid*. <ul><li>Why does Julian think the people on the train are mermaids?</li><li>Discuss the next three underwater pages; what is happening?</li><li>Why are the mermaids waving goodbye to Julian?</li><li>When Julian transforms, how do you think he is feeling?</li><li>What does Julian think Nana is going to say when she discovers him?</li><li>Julian is looking in the mirror when Nana walks away to get something. Look at Julian's face; what is he feeling?</li><li>Why does Nan give Julian a necklace? What does this show us about Nana?</li><li>When Nana first shows Julian the mermaid parade, he hides behind the corner; why?</li><li>When Julian and Nana join the parade, how do you think Julian is feeling?</li></ul>
Role play: Explore the role Nan plays in this story. Nan has a choice when she sees Julian dress up; she could choose to tell him off and make him take everything off (after all, he's using her curtains!). However, she instead chooses to help Julian dress up and she then takes him to meet more people dressing up. Why does she make that choice? What do you think she would say if people told her she was wrong to accept Julian and his mermaid clothes?   Ask for a volunteer to be Nan in role. We are going to ask Nan questions about her choices and Nan's job is to explain why she is choosing to be accepting. Sit Nan at the front of the room and encourage children to ask Nan questions. Nan could wear a hat or a headscarf to be in role. If children are not forthcoming give out cards with some question examples e.g. <ul><li>What did you think when you saw Julian dressed as a mermaid?</li><li>Were you cross about the curtains?</li></ul>

Table 4.6 (continued)

- Do you think Julian is happy?

- Why did you give Julian a necklace?

- What will you say if people are unkind about Julian?

- Why did you take Julian to the parade?

- What were you trying to show Julian at the parade?

- What do you want Julian to think about difference as he grows up?

Activity: The art work in this book is great stimulus for an art session. Alternatively children could create an identity poster showing different parts of Julian's identity – mermaid, schoolboy, footballer, mathematician, brother, etc.

Children could create a poster for Julian with the title 'Be who you want to be' or a poster with the title 'At our school we accept each other' and images of different children.

Plenary: Look at the picture of Nan where she first sees Julian as a mermaid; what is she thinking? Is she surprised? What do we think she is going to do when she says, 'Come here, honey.'

Nan is accepting even though at first, she is surprised. Nan chooses to accept Julian and his choices. She doesn't try to change her grandson; why not?

What do we know about Nan from this story?

Why might Julian feel like outsiders at the beginning of this story? Who makes sure Julian does not feel like an outsider? What can we do in our school to make sure no one feels like an outsider?

No Outsiders: everyone different, everyone welcome: Year 5

Table 5.1 To consider consequences

Text: *Kenny Lives With Erica and Martina* by Olly Pike
Learning intention: To consider consequences
Success criteria: I know what a consequence is/I know that all actions have consequences/I know that I have a choice in behaviour I join in and behaviour I choose to not to join in
Starter: What is a consequence? Give an example of a consequence. If a friend says, 'Go and call that boy a racist name,' what are the consequences of choosing to follow the instruction, and what are the consequences of choosing not to follow the instruction?
Main: Read *Kenny Lives With Erica and Martina*. Stop at the part where the neighbours take down the brick wall expecting Jenny and Hasan to come out. Ask children to discuss and predict how the story is going to end. Then read the end and discuss: why have Jenny and Hasan gone? Why did Kenny choose to build the wall back?
Role play: Look at the sections of the story where the people start shouting at Jenny and Hasan and study the language they use: write the sentences on the board: • 'You don't belong here' • 'We don't want you on our street!' • 'You are too different.' • 'You'll change everything.' • 'You are different and frightening.' Discuss possible responses to hearing the language; we all have options in our response, we could ignore it, walk away, join in or disagree. Ask children in pairs to explore responses to the language and feed back to the class. If that language was directed at you, what would you want people to say?
Activity: Kenny chose to build the wall again but graffiti a message on it, hoping Jenny and Hasan might see it. Why did Kenny paint 'Everyone is welcome' on the wall? What else could he paint? Children sketch a brick wall and using colours design their own graffiti message for Jenny and Hasan. Think about responses to the words they were hearing during the story.
Plenary: What is the message in this story? Can you think of a real-life example like this? Revisit the learning intention, why is this story about consequences? Why is this story about No Outsiders?

No Outsiders: everyone different, everyone welcome: Year 5

Table 5.2 To justify my actions

Text: *Rose Blanche* by Ian McEwan and Roberto Innocenti
Learning intention: To justify my actions
Success criteria: I know sometimes we have to make difficult decisions/I can justify my actions
Starter: Show a google-image of Jewish children in the Second World War. What is happening in the picture?/Why?/Who were the Nazis?/How did the Nazis justify their actions at the time?
Main: Read *Rose Blanche*. How do you know the book is told from a child's perspective? Where are the lorries in the story going? What are they carrying? Why? Explain concentration camps were set up in World War 2 in Germany and Poland to remove people who were Jewish and also any people who were different to the Nazis (disabled, gay, anyone who disagreed). Millions of people were killed.   What does Rose do in the story? Why does she do that? How do you think her mother would have felt if she found out? What would the soldiers do to Rose and her family if they found out? What happens to Rose at the end of the story? Look at the language in the last paragraph: 'Fresh grasses advanced across the land. There were new explosions of colour. Trees put on their bright new uniforms.' What does the author want to convey in this language?
Role play: Put children in to pairs. One is Mum and one is Rose. Mum has found out Rose is taking food to the children in the concentration camp and is waiting for her when she gets back one day. Role play the conversation between Mum and Rose. Rose should justify why she is doing that; what does Mum feel?
Activity: Rose's actions are very brave. Why does she risk her life to do that? Write a letter from Rose to a friend explaining what she has discovered and how it makes her feel; describe what she has chosen to do and why.
Plenary: If Rose had written a letter describing her actions in Nazi Germany what would have happened? In the prison what was the effect on the prisoners of Rose's kindness? Did she do the right thing? How can we make sure that situations like this never happen again where we live?

No Outsiders: everyone different, everyone welcome: Year 5

Table 5.3 To consider responses to racist behaviour

Text: *Mixed* by Arree Chung
Learning intention. To consider responses to racist behaviour
Success criteria: I understand what racism is/I can recognise racist behaviour/I know what to do if I hear or see someone being racist.
Starter: What is racism? Come up with a class definition. (racism is where someone is treated differently because of the colour of their skin or because of where they come from)
Main: Read *Mixed*; stop at points in the story to discuss following questions and predict what comes next: • The first time a Red shouts, 'Reds are the best!' how do the other colours react? (Look at their faces) • Look at the faces of the different colours when they divide the town; why are they looking so sad? • 'Life felt so vibrant!' what does this mean? • Why were the other colours unhappy about Blue and Yellow being friends? • Why was Blue and Yellow's child the colour green? • Why did the town tear down the walls? • What did the colours learn at the end of the story?
Role play/art activity: When Red first shouts 'Reds are best!', compare the responses of the Blues and Yellows. Does either response change the situation? Why not? Role play with two volunteers the Red shout and the Yellow response; why doesn't the Yellow response change the situation? (the Yellow response is no better than the Red behaviour). With two different volunteers role play the Blue response; why doesn't the Blue response change the situation? (ignoring the situation has no effect) Why does no one tell Red they disagree? When no one puts another point a view across, what happens to the town? How can we stop the colours putting up walls? What could Blues and Yellows do at this point in the story to stop the walls going up? (they could work together and persuade the reds to change their mind). We need to show the Reds that we can work together. Put the class in to groups of three and give each person a colour to work with (red, blue, green). Each group to create a poster to show the three colours working together successfully. They can use words and images, but the aim is to show the three colours united.
Plenary: What is the word that describes Red's behaviour? Red is being racist because he is judging a group of people by their skin colour. Red thinks he can only be with people who are the same colour. What does Red learn at the end of the story? If you hear someone behaving like Red, what can you do? If you don't feel able to speak up at the time, who can you tell? Remember, not everyone understands about or agrees with No Outsiders, but anyone can change their mind. If you hear someone saying something like 'Reds are best,' what can you say? You need to tell them about No Outsiders. Tell them about our school/town and how we're all different – different skin, different religion, different families, but we all get on and it works!

No Outsiders: everyone different, everyone welcome: Year 5

Table 5.4 To recognise when someone needs help

Text: *How To Heal a Broken Wing* by Bob Graham
Learning intention: To recognise when someone needs help
Success criteria: I know people have different life experience/I can empathise with others
Starter: Put up word 'empathy' on board – in partners come up with a definition
Main: Read text. What are the themes in the story? Discuss in talk partners and feed back. Once everyone has fed back read the postscript at the end about Amnesty. Now partners talk again about what the book might be about. Explain Amnesty International helps people around the world who are in prison because they speak up about wanting freedom of speech and democracy. Discuss the meaning of these terms. Explain in the UK we have freedom of speech and democracy but in some countries people are not allowed to vote or disagree with the government. Amnesty helps people who are in prison and can't tell their story by speaking up for them.   Read the book again and ask the children to think about what the bird represents. When 'No one looked' what does that mean? Why didn't the bird ask for help from the people around it? Because it had no voice so the boy stopped and spoke up for it. If the boy had walked on, what would have happened to the bird? What was the effect on the bird when the boy stopped and helped?
Role play: Give the sum cards out to the children. No one should show their card to anyone else. Explain most of the sums are easy to work out in your head and we are going to go around the circle saying the sum and the answer. However if you are not sure of your answer you need to think about your options. You could say, 'I can't do it', you could say, 'I'm not doing it', or you could ask for help when it is your turn. Make the point here that if someone gets a sum wrong what do we do? Do we laugh or do we help? You are looking to see who gives each other respect. Go round the circle and ask children to give their answers. When you get to the child with the difficult sum praise children who help/offer solutions. (You could have more than one difficult card).
Activity: There are many pages in the book with no words. Select a page and ask children to write a descriptive piece of writing about the image. Encourage use of feelings/emotion words.
Plenary: How did the role play feel? How did it feel to have an easy sum? How did it feel to have a difficult sum? Were you worried about how people might react when you couldn't do it? How would you have felt if no one had offered help? If you see someone needs help, what can you do? Why might they not ask for help? How can we make sure in our class everyone knows it is okay to ask for help? Return to empathy definition – do we want to change it?

No Outsiders: everyone different, everyone welcome: Year 5

Table 5.5 To explore friendship

Text: *The Girls* by Lauren Lee and Jenny Lovlie
Learning intention: To explore friendship
Success criteria: I know what friends are/I know how important friendship is/ I know sometimes friendship can go wrong/I value the people around me
Starter: Put images on the board of groups of friends. Show a range of ages and genders. Ask the children what they see. If the children say the people are friends, ask how they know. Can adults be friends? How long do people stay friends? Think about the friends you have in this class, was anyone a friend before you were in this class? Think about the person in your life you have been friends with the longest.
Main: Read *The Girls* and discuss: • The tree 'grew little girls as well as apples' what does this mean? • The girls were, 'as different as they were the same' what does this mean? • Sometimes the girls fell out; how did they become friends again? • Why does celebrating the success of someone else make you a good friend? • 'The branches spread wider and the roots reached deeper in to the ground' • What does this show is happening to the girls and their friendship? • 'When one heart was broken they all felt the pain' how does that happen? • The girls grow up, what keeps their friendship going?
Role play/activity: Talk about how the girls in the story grew up and their lives changed; they all became different people, had different jobs and houses and families, but they remained friends and supported each other. In groups of four children create four characters and plot their lives from now to adulthood. On a large piece of paper begin at the top by drawing the four friends and naming them, then develop a mind map of their lives, showing how they grow up and do some things that are different and some things that are different. Show how there are some activities that the four friends do together and identify what it is that keeps the friendship going. Revisit the last quarter of the book to see the achievements from each of the women in the story; what are the achievements going to be for your characters? Or In pairs, or individually, create a friendship map for two imaginary children as they go through childhood and adulthood.
Plenary: In the dedications at the start of the book, Lauren says, 'For my girls who made me the woman I am' and Jenny says, 'To all the strong women who have made me who I am.' What can we see about the authors from these lines; what does 'made me who I am' mean? Do you think the authors have friends like those shown in the book? The line 'as different as they were the same' is written twice, at the beginning and at the end of the story; why do you think the author has used the line two times? Why is this story about No Outsiders?

No Outsiders: everyone different, everyone welcome: Year 5

Table 5.6 To exchange dialogue and express an opinion

Text: *And Tango Makes Three* by Justin Richardson and Peter Parnell
Learning intention: To exchange dialogue and express an opinion
Success criteria: I know there are different ideas about equality around the world/I can exchange dialogue and express my opinion
Starter: Show the cover of *And Tango Makes Three* and tell the children you are going to read them a story that has been banned in some places. What does 'banned' mean? Log on to a book shop on the board and show the class that the book is available in the UK without problem; it's not banned here and it is available in libraries across the country. But in Hong Kong the government think this book is not suitable for children to read. You have to ask for it with an adult. The same has happened in Singapore. In 2006 libraries in Missouri, USA removed the book from their shelves. Ask the children, why do they think the book might have been banned? Are there any clues on the cover? Do you think it's ok to read it here?
Main: Read the book. Ask the children to discuss in pairs why they think some parents think the book should be banned.
Activity: Ask children to write responses to these three questions: • What is the story about? • Why are some people saying the book should be banned? • What do you think? Explain children can write whatever response they wish; there are not right or wrong answers to the questions and the aim of the lesson is to exchange dialogue and express an opinion; children can decide for themselves and write what they think as long as they back up their decision with explanations.
Plenary: Can animals be gay? Discuss and then read the author note about the story being true. What does the law say about LGBT+ people? Some people say they don't agree with people being LGBT+ and some say their religion says it is wrong to be LGBT+. There are different ideas around the world and in different communities, but we can still have respect for each other even if we disagree. Why is this story about No Outsiders?

No Outsiders: everyone different, everyone welcome: Year 6

Table 6.1 To consider responses to immigration

Text: *King of the Sky* by Nicola Davis
Learning intention: To consider responses to immigration
Success criteria: I know what immigration means/I know what empathy means/ I can empathise with a person in a different situation to me.
Starter: What does immigration mean? Why might a person immigrate? How can immigration affect a person? What do you think it feels like to start a new life in a new town with a different language and culture?
Main: Read *King of the Sky*. Stop as you go through the book to ask questions and discuss: <ul><li>In the first three pages (up to Rome) what do we find out about the boy?</li><li>How are Mr Evans and the boy different, how are they similar?</li><li>What do we find out about Mr Evans as the story unfolds?</li><li>Why do you think Mr Evans has such faith in the pigeon with the milk-white head?</li><li>Why do you think Mr Evans enters the milk-white pigeon into a race from Rome?</li><li>'A part of me was going with him. I wasn't sure it would come back' what is the boy thinking?</li><li>Why do you think the author chose to create a storm for racing day?</li><li>'Get out there boy AND WELCOME HIM' – what is the boy learning?</li><li>'The boy knew at last that he was home' – does the author mean the pigeon or the boy?</li></ul>
Activity 1: Consider how the boy feels throughout the story and what events affect his emotions. Create a story line showing the main events in the text and show how each event impacts on the boy.
Activity 2: Write a character description for the boy and for Mr Evans. Compare and contrast their characters, experiences and their roles in the story.
Activity 3: Write diary entries for the boy using the major events in the story – his arrival in Wales, meeting Mr Evans, learning about pigeons, building up for the big race, waiting for the pigeon to return, the return of the pigeon. Show the boy developing in confidence through his diary.
Plenary: The boy is an immigrant; he comes from Rome to live in Wales. Why is this difficult for him at first? Why does the description of the town make the boy think 'This is not where you belong'? Why do you think Mr Evans helps the boy? Why doesn't Mr Evans tell the boy to go away?   What was Mr Evans trying to show the boy? What can we learn from Mr Evans? What can we learn from the boy?   What is the message in this story? Why is this story about No Outsiders?

No Outsiders: everyone different, everyone welcome: Year 6

Table 6.2 To consider language and freedom of speech

Text: *The Only Way Is Badger* by Stella J. Jones and Carmen Saldana
Learning intention: To consider language and freedom of speech.
Success criteria: I know what freedom of speech means/I know how language can be used to persuade people/I know how important pupil voice is
Starter: What does freedom of speech mean? Explain it is the freedom to say what you think. Can words hurt people? What if someone says a group of people should be hurt – is it always ok for people to say what they think?
Main: Read *The Only Way Is Badger* and stop at points in the story to discuss the following questions: • How does Badger make other animals listen to him? • Discuss the language Badger uses such as 'I'm only trying to help you' – why is this effective? • When Badger starts chanting 'No deer here' what is the impact on a) deer b) other animals? • Why does Badger interrupt Moose when he says, 'I really think..' • When Badger instructs the animals to bark, why does rabbit say, 'I don't like where this is going?' what is rabbit realising? • Why does Badger end up alone? • What does Badger learn at the end of the story
Role play: By the end of the story the forest is empty; Badger has made everyone an outsider. At the end of the story he changes his mind and hopefully he has learned it's ok to be different, but many animals had to leave their homes during this story. How will these events affect the animals in the forest? When would have been the best time to stop this happening? Look at the very start of the story – how does it all begin? Give children the lines that Badger says on the first two or three pages; in the story the animals comply, but what other options are there when we hear people saying these lines? Ask children to consider responses and reply to Badger; speak up, use pupil voice and change the outcome of the story.
Activity: The ending is very quick. Does Badger really understand or is he only changing his behaviour because all his friends have left? What happens next? Do you think the animals accept Badger? Continue the story to show what happens next and show how the animals make sure this never happens again, or devise a lesson plan for young animals in the forest school to teach about diversity and difference so that this never happens again.

Table 6.2 (continued)

> **Plenary:** Consider freedom of speech – what is it? Should Badger have freedom of speech? Do you think if we had a discussion with Badger at the start, we could have changed his mind or maybe stopped animals having to leave? If Badger believed all deer should be killed, should he be allowed to say that? Would Badger just change his mind by himself? How do people change their minds? How do we get people to hear and think about different ideas? What is freedom of speech? Should everyone have freedom of speech? Is there a time when someone should be denied freedom of speech?

No Outsiders: everyone different, everyone welcome: Year 6

Table 6.3 To overcome fears about difference

Text: *Leaf* by Sandra Dieckmann
Learning intention: To overcome fears about difference
Success criteria: I can accept and work with people who are different to me/I can explore difference without fear/I can look for solutions to challenging situations
Starter: Discuss the success criteria; what does it mean? How can it be relevant to us in school? Look at the front cover of the book; what do you see, what do you notice about the animal and the habitat? What do you think this story might be about?
Main: Read *Leaf* and stop during the story to ask children in pairs to discuss the reaction of the animals to the polar bear, also to discuss what the polar bear might be doing with the leaves. Why do the animals have such a negative and fearful reaction to the polar bear? What changes the animals' opinions?
Role play: In the story Leaf is an outsider; Leaf doesn't try to talk to the other animals: why not? Look at the page where the animals are talking and using words like Monster, Huge, Needs to go. Who has the power in this situation and why? (the animals have power because there are more of them and they are safe). Focus on how we could change this situation. In pairs come up with points for a discussion to encourage the animals to find a solution. Think about what you can say to persuade them; it's not enough to say 'Just listen to Leaf'. (encourage children to think about the Equality Act and protected characteristics used to ensure equality perhaps use the protected characteristics that the animals may have, to show they are all different yet they all belong)
Activity: Create a sketch of the animal meeting where they discuss reasons for and against talking to him (he is dangerous/he is lost). Label each animal and identify differences for each to show that despite their own differences, they live and work together. Our aim is to demonstrate that Leaf also has differences and that means he fits in: we all have differences.
Plenary: The last line says the animals would tell the story to everyone so that 'No polar bear would ever get lost again'. What other reason is there for the animals to tell this story? What have they learned through this experience? (to accept difference, to avoid prejudice, to find solutions, to work together) Why do some people show prejudice to others? What can I do when I hear someone showing prejudice? Why is this about No Outsiders?

No Outsiders: everyone different, everyone welcome: Year 6

Table 6.4 To consider causes of racism

Text: *The Island* by Armin Greder
Learning intention: To consider causes of racism
Success criteria: I know what prejudice is/I know what can happen if racism is not challenged/I know how to challenge racist behaviour
Starter: Put the word 'racism' on the board. Children in pairs draw mind map and discuss what it is/what is the cause. Feed back ideas to class.
Main: Read *The Island*. Describe the character of the man washed up on the beach. What is the reaction of the people on the island? On one of the early pages there is an image of children pointing sticks at another child; what are they doing and why? Why didn't the man stay in the goat pen? Everyone gave a reason why the man couldn't work with them – why? List the rumours that were spread about the man; why do you think he eats bones with his hands? What is the role of the Fisherman? What happened to him as a result? What do you think happens to the man at the end? Why do the people build a wall? Is there a message in this story? What is it?
Role play: Say we are going to concentrate on the role of the Fisherman. On each table give out cards; half are blank and half have a fish. Children with a fish card take on the role of the Fisherman whose job it is to stand up for the man; other children in the group should use the arguments listed in the book. Can the Fishermen convince anyone? Ask some of the Fisherman to feed back to the class some of their arguments and how it felt to stand up for the man; did they convince anyone to change their mind?
Activity: Draw a cartoon strip telling the story of the Island. Limit your cartoons to six images, children to ensure they include the main features of the story. Include language from the book
Plenary: Talk about the wall built around the island – what will be the consequence of having a wall? The people will never meet anyone different to them. How will that affect their lives? Where does racism come from? Will the wall help or hinder the people to overcome racism? Have you heard any racist comments in our school? How can you respond if you hear comments based on prejudice? What does our school ay about racist behaviour?

No Outsiders: everyone different, everyone welcome: Year 6

Table 6.5 To show acceptance

Text: *Introducing Teddy* – Jessica Walton and Dougal MacPherson
Learning intention: To show acceptance
Starter: What does the word transgender mean? When we are born, we are assigned a gender; we are told, "You are a boy" or, "You are a girl." If someone is trans, as they grow older what is different?
Main: Read and discuss the story. One day Thomas doesn't feel like playing; what does Errol do? Why doesn't Thomas tell Errol what the worry is? Why does Thomas think Errol won't want to be friends? Stop the story when Thomas tells Errol about being a girl teddy and discuss/predict responses from Errol. Stop the story when Ava is told; what do you think Ava will say?
Discussion: Discuss the responses from Errol and Ava; what did you think they were going to say? What do you think of their responses? What did Tilly need to hear? How did their responses affect Tilly? Discuss the cover of the book; what is that about?
Activity: Write a letter to Tilly. Think about how Tilly feels in the story and how your words could affect her. Do you want Tilly to feel welcome in our school? Is Tilly frightened? Why? What does she need to hear? What can you write to make sure Tilly does not feel like an outsider?
Plenary: What can we learn from Errol? Is this book about being trans, or about friendship, acceptance, non-judgement?

No Outsiders: everyone different, everyone welcome: Year 6

Table 6.6 To consider democracy

Text: A *Day in the Life of Marlon Bundo* by Marlon Bundo and Jill Twiss
Learning intention: To consider democracy
Success criteria: I know what a democracy is/I know that we live in a democracy/ I know how laws are made/I know how laws can change.
Starter: Show a picture of Mike Pence. Explain who he is, where he is and about his job as Vice President of the USA. What does this mean? How did he become Vice President?   Explain the Pence family have a real pet rabbit called Marlon Bundo and he is famous. Mrs Pence and her daughter wrote a book about Marlon for charity called, 'Marlon Bundo's a day in the life of the Vice President'   Explain many LGBT people in USA believe Mike Pence does not support their human rights because in the past he did not support two men or two women marrying each other.
Main: Read A *Day in the Life of Marlon Bundo.*   • How do we know how Marlon feels about Wesley? • Who are the boring people in boring meetings? • Why do Wesley and Marlon want to get married? • What is the reaction of the other animals to the news? • What is the reason Stink Bug says Wesley cannot marry Marlon? • Why do the other animals decide to take a vote? • 'You are not in charge!' – what do you think of this response? • 'Stink bugs are temporary, love is forever' – why did the author choose this as the last line? • Look at Stink Bug's argument; what do you think of it? Stop reading and go to Activity 1.   Read the rest of the story.
Activity 1: Children write a response to Stink Bug. Children may agree or disagree with Stink Bug's points, however they respond they need to come up with reasoned arguments to support their statements.   Children could develop a dialogue between Stink Bug and Wesley; how do you think Stink Bug would reply?   Once the responses are written, read the rest of the book.
Activity 2: Write a newspaper report announcing the vote that removes Stink Bug from office. The report should explain the background to the vote and include quotes from the other animals about what happened.
Plenary: Why do you think the author chose to write this book, what do you think were the aims?   Why is this story about No Outsiders?

Appendix

No Outsiders in Our School: Teaching the Equality Act in Primary Schools was published in 2015 and provides a detailed guide to introducing the ethos in a school. Guidance includes working with governors and holding parent meetings. The chapter 'Simple answers to challenging questions' provides guidance for navigating difficult questions from parents. There is also a chapter on coming out in primary schools. The scheme of work includes lesson plans for 18 picture books that are not included in this new resource that can be used to extend a school's No Outsiders library.

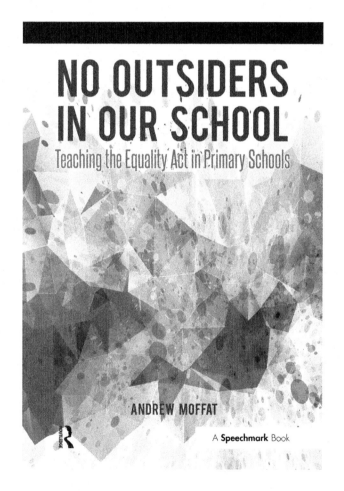

Reclaiming Radical Ideas in Schools: Preparing Young Children for Life in Modern Britain was published in 2017 and today Andrew claims to feel embarrassed by the title. 'The title is misleading,' Andrews says; 'I was trying to be clever but I wish I'd just called it 'Open No Outsiders lessons: teaching children and parents together' because that's what the book is about.' The book includes 13 lesson plans for open lessons where parents join their child for a No Outsiders workshop. Andrew piloted these lessons in his own school and one of the chapters speaks honestly about the successes of the pilot alongside changes that were made to the plans before publication. The aim is to develop the inclusive language used in school so that it can be used in the home too; we want parents to be as confident and enthusiastic as the children in their understanding

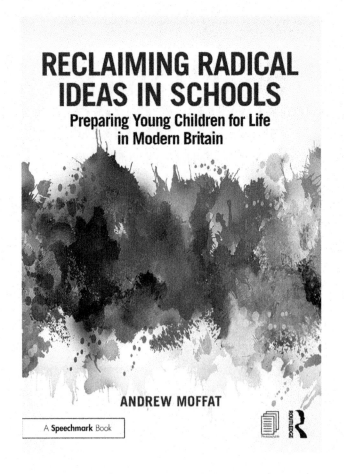

of equality. There are also chapters on reinforcing the ethos around school and on using the No Outsiders ethos as a framework when responding to news of terrorist attacks. In summer 2018 Andrew led a number of No Outsiders open sessions in Birmingham libraries using the plans in this book. There is a short film on YouTube documenting this (www.youtube.com/watch?v= TsG-byFlfTY).

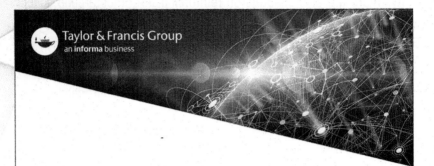